Surviving Life as a
Dumbass

Surviving Life as a **Dumbass**

Michael E. Webster

iUniverse, Inc.
New York   Bloomington

Three Years Ago

I guess today's the day. It's been a long time coming. I thought I might feel different when it finally arrived. I thought I might feel *something* anyway. I guess all my training has prepared me, because I really feel nothing but calm. I know you won't understand, and I really don't know if I can explain it to you. It's taken me years to get to this point, so I really can't expect you to understand my journey by reading this. I guess all I can do is tell you the story and let you draw your own conclusion.

I'll start by telling you how I've made my living for the last thirty plus years. I am a pharmacist. I usually don't tell people that if they ask what I do. Usually I say I'm a martial arts instructor. Actually, the combination of being a pharmacist and teaching martial arts got me to this day. Why don't I want to tell that I'm a pharmacist? Pharmacy has changed so much over the last thirty years that I just don't want to be associated with it. I really don't consider it a "profession" anymore. Pharmacy was a profession in the past. People respected it, and you could actually treat a person as a patient instead of a customer. Those days are long gone. That was before public aid, a thousand different insurance companies, television advertising, coupons, giving away medication, chain pharmacies on every other corner, and pharmacies in every grocery and department store. All of those factors had the profession on the way down, and then drive-ups finished it off. Although it pays well, it's just a glorified fast food job. People are getting grocery sacks full of medicine. The drugs are keeping them alive twenty years longer, most of which they spend in nursing homes getting even more drugs. I can't see that I'm helping anyone.

I've worked in just about all areas of pharmacy in the last thirty years. I've worked for independents, chain stores, the VA, my own stores, a grocery store, and now for a department store. So I've covered the full range of pharmacy. The only reason I made it this long was studying martial arts. By doing that, I had an outlet for the frustrations of my work. There are few if any good jobs left in pharmacy. My present job was bearable for a year or so, but then they moved the pharmacy up front and put in a drive-up. The manager took a job with Walgreens, so the job is changing again. I just don't want to do it anymore. It is still several years until I can retire. So that's what got me to this day.

Today is the day I die. My belief of death is not what most people would consider normal. Death is like the past. You can do nothing to change or stop it. You can't control where or when you're born, most of your life is beyond your control, but to some degree you can control when and how you die. I know few people, if any, who can say that they've done everything they've wanted to do in their life. Well, I can. I've done some unbelievable things. Like the samurai, I've considered myself a dead man for quite a while. I've decided that I've done enough, and it's time for me to go. Today is Sunday. My wife Peggy goes to visit her father on Sundays, and she doesn't get home until late. I haven't eaten anything for a couple of days. I know it's silly, but I don't want to leave a mess when I die. That's why I've decided the shower is the best place to do it. I am not depressed. In fact, I'm in a pretty good mood.

A few of the people I work with are here to watch their favorite television shows on my big screen. They brought some beer and wine, and I drink some with them. We're having fun, and I lose track of the time. The phone rings. It's Peggy. She doesn't know the people here.

"I'm starting to leave here. I should be home in a couple of hours. Who's making the noise?"

"It's some people from work. We're watching the shows they like. They're just having fun."

"You sound like you've been drinking. Have you? That's just great. I thought you knew better."

"I haven't had that much. It won't matter anyway." She hangs up on me. The other people can tell from my conversation that something is wrong.

"Is she mad because we're here?"

"No, she's just mad at me because I've been drinking." They really don't believe me, so they get their things and leave. I assure them again that she isn't mad at them, only me. When they leave, I get a knife and go to the shower. It'll be over within about three minutes. It would have been, but I've had enough to drink to make me stupid. Instead of getting it over quickly like I planned, I decide that I want to think over my life. I turn the radio up high on the oldies station and get in the shower. Music brings back old memories. I make a deep, three-inch-long cut on both arms. The veins are bigger here than at the wrist. I sit on a seat in the shower watching the blood go down the drain, thinking over my life. I think I've done my best to make up for all the bad things I have done. I don't know how long I've been in here. The alcohol has screwed up my sense of time. A lot of blood has gone down the drain. I'm getting cold, and I have to brace my feet to keep from sliding off the seat. What's the song playing now? "Maggie May"—that's it. I must have heard that song a thousand times the summer I went back to school. All I had was a radio in my apartment when Peggy met me. Shit! She's going to be really mad at me. Damn, I hope she doesn't think this is her fault. I don't want her thinking that the last thing she said to me made me do this. What time is it? Is she home yet? Peggy. *Peggy*! There's no answer. Maybe I really didn't yell for her. It's getting hard to think. Maybe it's all in my head. Oh well, I tried. Damn, how much blood do I have in me? It can't be long now.

The shower door opens. It's Peggy. "Mike. What have you done?"

"Don't be mad at me. Please don't be mad at me."

"Let me have the knife. Give me the knife, Mike."

"Just let it end. It's almost over now."

"You don't want to do this. Please give me the knife and let me help you." Shit. I can't continue now. I give her the knife. She turns the shower off and helps me stand. She gets me to the chair and tries to stop the blood flow. "I don't suppose you'll let me take you to the ER."

"No. If you can't fix it then let me alone."

"Keep these towels pressed on the cuts. I've got to go get some bandages. Keep pressure on it. I won't be gone long. You are going to do that. Is that right?"

"Alright I'll do it. I've already screwed it up." While she's gone, all I think about is what a dumbass I am. I let the alcohol screw my life up again. She's back already. She must have driven fast.

The cuts are deep, but they're straight with no hesitation marks. She manages to bandage them up pretty good. Now I've got to get some sleep. I have to work tomorrow. She manages to get me in bed. Sometime during the night I get up to go to the bathroom, and I fall through the shower doors. It makes quite a racket. It definitely wakes her up

"What happened? Are you alright?"

"It seems I fell down again, so I've got to get up. I'm really tired of doing this."

"You think you're going to work tomorrow? You can't even stand up."

"I don't have a choice. I'm alive, so I've got to go to work." In the morning we change the bandages and I go to work wearing a long sleeve shirt. The cuts keep seeping through the bandages, and I have to go to the restroom to dry my shirt sleeves. The only people I tell are the manager, who is leaving, my tae kwon do students, and my friend, "Preacher." I don't want everyone making a big deal out of it. It's another experience that my students can learn from. It didn't kill me, so it made me stronger. I've got to use it as a learning experience. At least that will give it a purpose.

One and a Half Years Ago

"**M**ike. Mike!"

"What?"

"Turn over."

"Turn over what?"

"Get off your back. You're breathing funny."

"Shit."

I'm finally awake enough to realize what's going on. Although it hurts most every part of my body, I force myself to slowly turn on to my right side. When I look at the alarm clock it reads 6:15 AM. My mind tries to remember what day it is, and if I have to go to work. I do, so that means I have to get up in fifteen minutes. I've been awake most of the night. I remember that the last time I looked at the clock it was 4:35 AM. I finally go to sleep, and she wakes me up because I'm breathing funny! This thought pisses me off, but just waking up pisses me off. I really would like to just not wake up. There's no sense trying to go back to sleep for fifteen minutes, so I turn off the alarm clock and slowly force my body to get up.

I do remember to turn off the house burglar alarm. Guess my mind is functioning, if not my body. The intense workouts are taking their toll on me. Going down the stairs is a slow and painful process. I take one slow step at a time holding on to both banisters. I know how it feels to fall down the stairs. I've done it more than once. Finally down, I start sorting out my pills. There are eight of them: two for blood pressure, two antidepressants, a pain tablet, a vitamin, a fish oil capsule, and a glucosamine tablet. I know I should eat something, but I'm not hungry. Eating seems like too much trouble. All of the food from the microwave tastes the same anyway. I just have a glass of milk with my eight pills—so much for breakfast.

My body is starting to loosen up some, so the trip back up the stairs is not as bad as coming down. My morning routine is pretty much ingrained in my mind, so I don't have to think too much. First I brush my teeth. About half the teeth in my mouth are caps or bridges. Sometimes I think of the fight or other reasons they're there. When I'm shaving, it's hard to believe it's me in the mirror. A lot of the scars have faded, but I can still see them. The image in the mirror shows the years of abuse. My eyes are still blue but faded, and the pain shows through them. Sometimes I really hate the person in the mirror looking back at me. I think, *why did I have to wake up and do this again?* I never see a smiling person in the mirror. I hardly ever laugh or smile anymore. Then my mind tells me to forget it and get into the shower.

Hot water is the only thing that takes away my physical pain, or at least makes it bearable. I miss the hot tub in my old house. I had built a room off of the bedroom just for the hot tub. I got in it the first thing every morning, and before going to bed every night. The shower is the next best thing. As the hot water runs over my body, the pain pill starts to kick in and I can move a lot easier. There's one weird thing I can't figure out. I don't sing in the shower, but there's always a song running through my mind. It's never the same song. It's generally an old song or a country western tune. At first I thought it was the song that came on with my alarm, but it still happens on the mornings I get up without the alarm. I stopped trying to figure it out. I'm usually showered, dressed, and on my way to work in less than thirty minutes.

I always go in twenty to thirty minutes early so I can get started on the prescriptions people have put on the computer during the night. I don't like starting out in the hole. My military training still affects me. We always relieved the watch fifteen minutes early, so the person on watch could tell us what we needed to know and get off watch. There's no excuse for being late.

One morning not long ago started out as another rewarding day in the pharmacy. I told a patient that it was too soon to refill his prescription. Maybe he had brought the wrong bottle, or maybe he had some at home. Later that day, he called the pharmacy, and the person who answered told me I was referred to as the "short dumb pharmacist."

As I thought about that the rest of the day, I began to wonder why I still do this job. The only reason is the money. I don't need it, but I give away a lot to others. There are plenty of people who need help to get their prescriptions, buy food, or go to school. A few years ago a chain I worked for had a twenty-five thousand dollar sign-on bonus for pharmacists, and they couldn't find anyone to take it. At that time, the Army also had a twenty-five thousand dollar sign-on bonus. They found people, and they get shot at! If you can't pay someone twenty-five thousand dollars to take a job that pays eighty thousand dollars, maybe that shows it's not such a great job.

Anyway, I had written a short four-page paper called "Short and Dumb," listing some of the things I have done in my life. I made sure the person who called me the "short, dumb pharmacist" got a copy of it. I knew the only thing that he would notice was that I was a martial arts master. For some funny reason, he now treats the pharmacy personnel with a lot more respect.

Everyone who read that paper liked it. Several people over the years have told me I should write a book. So I decided to tell you the story of my life. Maybe my story will make both of us understand why I don't like what I see in the mirror most days.

The Early Years

Stories that sailors tell are called "sea stories." Sea stories differ from fairy tales only in that fairy tales start with "Once upon a time," and sea stories begin with "This ain't no shit." My life seems like a cross between the two. I can't guarantee the accuracy of every detail. Much of this happened a long time ago, and some of it happened during long drunken periods of which I have little memory. I'll try to be as honest as I can—no shit!

Growing up in the '40s in Paoli, a small town in southern Indiana, wasn't overly exciting. I was the baby of the family. I had two older sisters who enjoyed playing tricks on their little brother. I had curly hair, and they would put me in dresses with ribbons in my hair and then take pictures of me. When I was older they took great delight in embarrassing me by showing the pictures to my friends or girlfriends. Thankfully my father (who was a barber) cut my hair short and the curls never came back.

Certain things stand out in my mind. We had an ice box instead of a refrigerator, and every few days a man would deliver ice. The outhouse was on the bank of the creek behind the house. My dad would grow tomato plants as tall as the back of the house. My most exciting memory was the day an airplane landed in the field across the creek when I was just five years old. The plane had some mechanical problem and made an emergency landing. The pilot was fixing the plane, and I bugged my mom until she took me over there to talk to him. I asked him a million questions, and he was really nice and tried to answer, even though they were dumb kid questions. He even let me sit in the plane, and I was totally awed by all the dials and gauges. I couldn't believe I was actually sitting in an airplane. When he had the problem fixed, he said something that literally made my mouth drop open.

"Would you like to take a ride?" I was so excited I almost peed my pants!

"Mom, can I? Please. I'll do anything. I'll be good forever!"

"Your dad would have a fit if he found out"

"I'll never tell. Cross my heart. Please."

"I'll probably regret this, but let's go."

So I went on my first airplane ride. I got in the seat next to the pilot and mom got in the back. He had both controls in, and he asked me if I wanted to take the wheel. I looked at him like he was crazy, and then looked at mom, who looked scared.

"Just hold the wheel steady. It'll be okay." So I did like he said, and it was unbelievable. I was flying an airplane! I knew then that I wanted to be a pilot. Little did I know that one day not only would I be flying airplanes, but also jumping out of them.

When I was five years old, we moved to a new house on the other side of town. It wasn't quite finished when we moved in. It was bigger than the old house. It had three bedrooms, a front room, a dining room, a kitchen, and a bathroom. My older sister had gone to nursing school before we moved, so my other sister and I would have our own rooms. I was scared the first night I had to sleep alone in my new room. I made mom leave the lamp on. She said "There's nothing in the dark that isn't there in the light." I still made her leave the light on for several nights until I was sure she was right. I had other questions about the new house.

9

"Why do you call the middle room a dining room? We eat in the kitchen."

"Some people eat in another room and not in the kitchen."

"Then where do they put their radio and stove and other stuff?"

"They have a room they call the family room."

"So why don't we call it the family room?"

"We just don't. Stop asking so many questions. You can call it what ever you want."

"Okay, but it still seems silly to me."

They were still digging the basement, and we still had to use an outhouse until the plumbing was done.

"Why do we need a basement? The other house didn't have one."

"That's where we'll put the coal, and the stove that heats the water. I'll do the laundry down there too."

"You mean we won't have to heat water to take a bath anymore?"

"When they're done, we'll have hot and cold water in the sinks and bathtub. There'll be water in the stool in the bathroom, and we won't have to go to the outhouse anymore."

"Won't it stink in here like the outhouse? That doesn't sound like a good idea to me."

"No, you'll flush the toilet and it'll go away. You're just going to have to wait and see."

This new house had another great thing about it. It was only a block behind the town's schools. I could see the kids having recess, and I couldn't wait until I could join them. We didn't have kindergarten then, so I was six before I could start school. I really hadn't been around too many kids my age before. I was looking forward to having someone to play with. I had learned to read before I began school from my mom reading comic books to me. I could also tell time and do basic math, so I had a pretty easy time in first grade. I wasn't bashful, and I generally volunteered to do any activity. I guess you could call me a teacher's pet. We got polio shots, and I made sure I was the first in line. The only bad memory I have of that year was when a boy bled to death when he was getting his tonsils taken out. When my sister came home on a weekend from nursing school, I asked her how and why they took out anyone's tonsils. I didn't even know what tonsils were. I can't remember what she told me, but I know it didn't sound like anything I would want to go through. From that time on, I suffered a lot of sore throats that I never told anyone about.

Starting school revealed a problem that I hadn't been aware of before. I have a speech defect, and so I have difficulty pronouncing *r, s,* and *th* sounds. It was much more pronounced when I was young. I was really hard to understand. There was only one black family in our town, and one of the kids, James, was in my class. At recess one day we were choosing sides to play ball. I was choosing for our side.

"I want James because he's bigger." He came running over to me and pushed me down.

"What did you say? Did you call me a nigger?" I got up and before I could say anything he hit me in the face and knocked me back down. I had never been hit like that before. When I started to get up he hit me again.

"You think you're better than me white boy? Get up and prove it."

This time I got up fast and hit him before he could hit me again. We continued fighting until a teacher came and broke it up.

"What's going on here? Why are you fighting?"

"I don't know. I picked him to be on my side and he came over and started hitting me," I said.

"He called me a nigger."

I looked at the teacher and said, "What's a nigger?" I don't think I had ever even heard the word nigger. Evidently, he had! She said it was a bad word to call a black person. When we all calmed down and things were explained, James and I were good friends from then on. In the third grade we had the same kind of boots, and he still remembers his mother telling him to be careful not to get them mixed up. He thought that was really funny since his feet were twice the size of mine. The speech defect was a problem, but since I made good grades and was good in sports, my classmates never made fun of me to my face.

I had a relatively normal childhood, but when I was in the fifth grade I had a pretty bad experience. My parents bought me a Red Rider BB gun for Christmas. Mom made me promise I would be careful, and not to shoot at birds with it. One afternoon I was shooting at tin cans when a couple of older kids from the neighborhood came up and wanted to shoot my gun. I let them, but they wanted to shoot birds. I told them they couldn't shoot birds, and I asked them to give me back the gun. They gave it back, but then they came up with another thing to shoot at. One had a safari helmet, and they wanted to see if it would stop a BB. One put the helmet over his face, and they both told me to shoot at it. I didn't want to do it, but they kept insisting it would be okay and to stop being a sissy. So I pulled the trigger. Just as I fired, he raised the helmet and was shot in the eye.

He ran down the alley screaming, "I'm blind! I'm blind!"

"You shot his eye out!"

"You made me do it," I said and started crying. I could still hear him screaming all the way from his house.

"I did not," said the other kid. He grabbed the helmet and took off running to his house.

I didn't know what to do. The screaming had stopped, but I couldn't think. I threw down the gun and went into the basement and sat in a corner crying. It seemed like a long time until I heard mom yelling for me. She and the other boy's mother finally found me.

"Did I blind him?"

"No, he's not blind. Why did you do that?"

"I didn't want to. They kept telling me to shoot. I'm sorry. I didn't want to hurt him. Am I going to jail? What's going to happen to me?"

"Wait till your dad gets home. Go to your room. Where's the gun?"

"I threw it down in the yard. I don't ever want to see it again."

His mother said that he had admitted it had been his idea, and she wasn't mad at me. The BB had gone into the corner of his eye and lodged inside his nose. The doctor dug it out, and I don't think his eye was severely damaged. It was sheer luck. I wasn't punished, but I never said much and refused to play with the other kids in the neighborhood for a long time after that. I don't know what they did with the gun, and I didn't care. I didn't want to ever see it again. Even though I knew that they had told me to do it, I was still the one who pulled the trigger. I guess that was the first time I realized that I had to take responsibility for my actions, and I had to accept the consequences.

By the sixth grade students were considered old enough to be school crossing guards. There were three crosswalks that were manned by crossing guards before and after school. Everyone wanted to be a crossing guard because they got out of class and got to wear cool badges. I was the captain, so my badge was blue and gold. I had to check on all the other guards to make sure they were doing their job. I admit it. I thought I was hot shit. That was when I discovered I liked being a leader.

Through high school I stayed mostly on the straight and narrow. I made good grades, played sports, was on the student council and in the National Honor Society. Peer pressure in school was not like it is now. There was smoking, drinking, and fighting, but nobody brought guns to school. Smoking was very common back then and all the other members of my family smoked. Maybe from that exposure and the black coal soot that filled my nose every morning from the coal stove heating our house, I was not drawn to smoking. I know I must have smelled of smoke, but I guess no one noticed since they all lived with it. Now I can smell a smoker from ten feet away. Smoking, however, is one of the few things I've never tried. It just never appealed to me, and it didn't go together with being an athlete.

The summer before my senior year I met a couple of guys who changed the course of my life. Most of my friends smoked and drank, but I had never tried alcohol until I met these guys. A new family had moved to town from Pennsylvania. They had twin sons named John and Dan. These guys were big and mean, and they weren't too happy to be living in a small town in southern Indiana. Their father was a big shot in some construction company. They worked for him, so they had to move with him despite the fact that they were twenty-two years old.

I met them at a drive-in restaurant called the Shake Burger that was the local hangout. They were parked across from me. They were far enough away that I could see their car, a '59 Corvette, but not who was in it. I hadn't been there ten minutes when these two big guys start walking toward my car. The first words they ever spoke to me were, "Why are you looking at us punk? You think we're cute? Maybe you'd like to get out of your car and change our looks?"

"I wasn't looking at you. I was looking at your car. Nobody in this town has a cool car like that. I think it's really great. I'd like to look at it closer, if you'll let me live long enough to enjoy it."

They just stared at me for a minute. I was pretty sure I was going to get my ass beat. Then they both laughed. One of them opened my door, and the other one snatched me out of my car like I was a rag doll. Each took one of my arms, and they hauled me over to their car. One of them reached into the car, and I thought he'd pull out something like a tire iron. What he pulled out was a can of beer.

"Have a beer. You look like you need one."

"I really don't drink, but I think you're right. I feel like I could really use one."

So I had my first beer, and that was the start of a strange friendship. To this day I don't know why we got along so well. They both dated girls who were friends of mine, but I don't think they liked any other guy in town. I spent most of my time with them instead of my other friends. They even let me drive their Corvette. They were the toughest guys I'd ever seen. They definitely had a great influence on me. I did what they did, and thus began my life of drinking and fighting.

The first really dumb thing drinking caused in my life happened on my graduation night. I was out with some guys from my class, got some whiskey, and drank most of it. We were driving out on a country road, and I told the driver to stop because I had to piss. Here's the really dumb part. I didn't wait for him to stop! I just opened the door and got out. He was going about thirty miles per hour. It was definitely a sobering experience. I tumbled several yards down the side of a gravel road until a tree stopped me. By the time they stopped and backed up, I was up and walking to the car. Everyone was surprised I was still alive, *including me*!

Besides looking like I'd been dragged through a gravel pit, the only actual injury I had was a rock buried in the palm of my left hand. It was buried so deep we couldn't get it out, so I had to have the doctor dig it out the next morning. I told my parents I'd fallen out of my friend's hay loft. I'm pretty sure only my mother believed me!

That afternoon we left on a seven day senior trip to Pittsburgh, Washington D.C., and New York. A classmate, who later became a nurse, changed my bandage every day. Although it's faded over the years like the memory, I still have a scar to remind me of that night.

High school was over, and I had no idea what I wanted to do with the rest of my life. Most of my friends were either going into the military or going to college. I would have joined the Marines, but I got a scholarship to Purdue. So I decided to try college, even though I didn't know what to study.

My parents had no money to help me. My father had to fill out a financial statement before I could get the scholarship money. He had earned only $3,300 that year. Even in 1962, that was not very much. It surprised me. Though I never got everything I wanted, I always had everything I needed. We didn't have a television until I was in the fifth grade, and even when I left for college in 1962 we didn't have a telephone. My father didn't waste money. He never bought anything on credit. If he couldn't pay cash for it, we didn't have it. I don't think he could have lived that way in today's world. I know it couldn't have been easy back then either. He lived and died not owing anything to anyone, and I respect him for that. He made me start working when I was thirteen, cleaning fence rows on our farm and for our neighbors. When I was old enough to get a work permit I worked at a grocery store. I didn't like him for making me do it, but it taught me to work and not expect others to support me.

There were three factories in town, and I worked at one of them for the summer to help pay my college expenses. The Paoli Handle Factory made hammer and hatchet handles, baseball bats, croquet sets, and other assorted wooden articles. It was hot, dirty, and boring work that paid minimum wage. I worked fifty hours and cleared fifty-four dollars a week after taxes. There was a man working next to me who had twelve kids, and he was making the same money. Maybe I didn't know what I wanted to do with my life, but I definitely didn't want to wind up like him. Thinking back on it now, I have to respect him too. Like my father, he worked hard for what he had, and didn't expect the state to support him.

By my second year of college I was just putting in my time, doing just enough to get by. I still didn't know I wanted to do. I had three friends in pharmacy school, and they talked me into trying that.

It was sometime during that second semester that I had another experience with alcohol that I was really lucky to have lived through. One weekend I went to Terre Haute to visit some friends who went to Indiana State. They wanted to get some booze and go to a drive-in movie. They took me to a bar, where I went in and bought some whiskey and vodka. They never even asked to see any kind of ID, even though I was only nineteen.

We went to the drive-in movie, and that was the last thing I remember. I woke up lying on a bed made of boards in a yellow brick room with a red wooden door. I was muddy, bloody, my clothes were torn, and I had shit and pissed my pants. I could hear people talking, so I thought maybe I was in a dorm room. I got up and tried to leave the room. The door wouldn't budge. I beat on it and kicked it, but it definitely wasn't going to open, so I started yelling for someone to open the door. Someone opened the door alright. It was a cop!

"Shut up!" he yelled.

"Where am I?" I asked.

"Vigo County Jail."

"What for?"

"Rape."

If I hadn't already shit my pants, I would have then. "I never raped anyone!" I said.

"How do you know?" he shot back, and shut the door. He was having fun messing with my mind. It definitely worked! He knew I had no idea what had happened. I could hear him laughing as he walked down the hall. He was right. I could not remember anything after entering the drive-in. I can't tell you all of the emotions running through my head at that moment, but if I had to rate my all time worst moments, that one definitely ranks high on the list.

After what seemed like hours, he came to let me out. My friends had come to pick me up. We went to their dorm where I took a shower, threw away my clothes, and found out what happened. After we were at the drive-in for a couple of hours, I had drunk most of the whiskey. A couple of the drive-in employees were going around checking cars. They thought someone had slipped in without paying, and they mistakenly decided it must be us.

There was an argument, and then a fight, with me doing most of the fighting. The cops were called, but I didn't give up quietly. When asked about the liquor, my friends said I stood up and said, "I bought it and I drank it, and I'll stand here till doomsday if you want." Then I fell on my face in the gravel. My friends confessed everything. Since they told the cops that I had bought the liquor, and where I had bought it, they were not taken to jail with me.

A month or so later I had to go to court in Terre Haute. The judge gave me a choice: jail time and a big fine, or testifying against the bar and bartender. Since everyone already knew the truth, I had to take the deal.

A few months later, we all had to go to a court in Indianapolis to testify against the bar and bartender. I don't know what sentence they received, but I know it couldn't have been good. I felt really bad about it. I know they broke the law, but I hated to see others suffer because of my stupid act. It was a really bad experience for everyone. My friends were never very friendly after that, and I couldn't really blame them. I didn't like myself very much then either. I finished the semester with only a C average. The first chapter of my life was coming to a close, and unfortunately, it was going to get worse. Why didn't I learn from these experiences? I had to know I was headed down the wrong road. I now know that wanting to change your life is easier than actually doing it. I think that somewhere in my mind I thought I would do the right thing. It's too bad that the dumbass part was still the strongest.

Look what they did to me!

Dad's tomatoes.

Clean-cut high school graduate (1962).

The Lost Years

I couldn't imagine spending another summer working at the handle factory to make money to return to a school that I didn't like. So I did what I'd always said I would do and joined the Marines. After I took the tests and had the physical, I was supposed to go to Indianapolis to be sworn in, and then I would be flown to boot camp. The Greyhound Bus came through Paoli to Indianapolis only a couple of days a week. The bus I was supposed to take was canceled for some reason, so I had to wait for the next one. Who would think that something as simple as a change of a bus schedule could change the course of your life? If I had taken that first bus I might not be writing now.

While I was waiting for the next bus, the Navy recruiter came to my house to talk to me. He said because of my two years of college, he could offer me pay grade E-3 (versus E-1) upon joining, and that he could guarantee me aviation and a chance at the NAVCAD (Naval Aviation Cadet) program.

I told him I had already joined the Marines, which he already knew. He said I could use all the paperwork done for them, and he'd drive me to Indianapolis that day.

I went to the Marine recruiter and asked if he could match that deal. He couldn't, so I took the Navy's offer. That was one pissed off Gunny Sergeant. He'd done all the work, and the Navy came and stole me from him.

They took me to Indianapolis that afternoon, and I stayed at the YMCA that night. The next day I was sworn into the Navy. As I repeated the oath, I wondered if I was doing a smart thing. I was turning my life over to someone else to decide my future for the next four years, and I wouldn't be able to quit. Unfortunately, I kept saying the words, and I now belonged to the Navy. I was put in charge of three other recruits while we were transferred to Chicago for transport to the Great Lakes Naval Training Center for boot camp. When we got to Chicago it was late in the day, and we were loaded on a bus with other recruits. It was the middle of the night when we got into boot camp. If I had doubts before, they were magnified a hundred times as we got off that bus. We were welcomed to the Navy in that special way that they have at all boot camps. I think everyone should have the experience of boot camp. Seeing it in movies or listening to stories just isn't the same. I know and understand why it's done the way it is. In fact, I think they're not tough enough nowadays. When you're there, however, the only thing you want is to get out. I was no different, and that led to my first bad decision.

By the start of our third week it seemed like we had been there three years. That was when we were offered a deal. The nuclear Navy was growing rapidly, and they needed nuclear trained personnel as soon as possible.

Here was the deal. If you volunteered for the nuclear program, you would be sent to a special nuclear company and given an advanced course in boot camp. You would be out in two more weeks. Then you would be sent to a class "A" school for your rate (job) training. Next you would go to nuclear power school, followed by nuclear prototype, followed by submarine school. Finally, you would be assigned to a fleet attack or missile nuclear submarine. The catch was that first you had to sign up for six years, since all the training took two years. Second, you had to qualify for this program based on tests given in boot camp. Third, the only rates available were machinist mate (MM) or boiler tender (BT). Last, if you washed out of any part, you still were held to a six-year enlistment. They wanted enough men to form two companies.

I told them about my NAVCAD guarantee. I was told I'd have to commit to six years for that anyway, and that I would still get that chance. I told them I had little mechanical ability, and they told me they would teach me everything I needed to know. Here was another turning point in my life. I knew I shouldn't let the officer persuade me to do this. I knew I would never be happy doing either of these jobs. But I wanted out of boot camp, and I convinced myself that it didn't matter. I was going to be a pilot. If I got out of boot camp faster I could get to NAVCAD sooner. He was right about the six-year commitment, and I would probably make the Navy a career if I was a fighter pilot. So in dumbass tradition, I signed on the dotted line.

I became a graduate of one of only two special nuclear companies to ever come out of boot camp with only five weeks of training. I was given a week's leave, and then I reported back to Great Lakes Naval Training Center for twelve weeks of my machinist mate "A" school. The bookwork in Machinist Mate School wasn't very hard for me. I studied little and aced all the tests. I didn't take it too seriously, since I thought I'd never be doing that job. We went to Milwaukee or Chicago most weekends, and I began shaping my drunken sailor image. While in Milwaukee, I got a tattoo of an eagle with an anchor and "USN." Back then only sailors or tough guys had tattoos. Now everyone has one.

Since I was an E-3, I was put in charge of my barracks. That's when I found out that leaders aren't always popular. After getting my ass chewed several times, I started enforcing the rules even if I had to get physical to do it. Being a nice guy didn't get the job done. So I had to change tactics and became a hard ass. I was definitely not liked. My nickname was "Fireman Freddie." "Fireman" was what the E-3 ranks were called and "Freddie" was just for the sake of alliteration. Most of the men didn't even know my name. I didn't blame them. I was an asshole. When it was lights-out I made sure everyone was in their bunks and quiet. I'd walk through the barracks and make sure it was quiet, or there would be consequences—which were being put on report or receiving an ass beating. In the mornings I'd take a Coke bottle and run it around the inside of a steel trash can. It made a horrible sound that definitely got them up. In future years, I learned how to compromise. I learned how to get the job done my way, but to let those above me think it was getting done their way. I became a kinder, gentler asshole who got the job done.

The Navy kept its promise. During "A" school, I was sent to Glenview Naval Air Station where I was given more written tests, more physicals, and an oral board evaluation by five officers to determine if I was officer material.

The first question they asked me was, "Do you know what APE is?"

While I was thinking Air Patrol Echelon and Aviation Pilot Exam, they said, "It's a big hairy animal."

The questions got more serious after that. I passed all of the tests, and I thought I was on my way. I was going to be a Navy fighter pilot—the best in the world. Then as usual, my life took a sudden wrong turn.

I was called back to Glenview. They wanted to check my eyes again. When they dilated my pupils, my right eye was not a perfect 20/20. It was close, but not close enough.

They gave me a choice, and we all know how I do with choices. I could fly helicopters, be a RIO (Radar Intercept Officer), or return to the nuclear program. The Navy had no combat helicopters, and taking RIO seemed like accepting second place. So I decided to stay with the nuclear sub program which would prove to be another really bad decision. I finished MM "A" school near the top of the class and was given orders to report to Nuclear Power School.

The Navy's Nuclear Power School was in Vallejo, California, south of San Francisco. I was off to sunny California! When I got there in late December 1964, it had been raining eighteen straight days. There was water everywhere, and it rained for another week or so. I should have taken it as an omen of my life to come.

At our introduction class, they told us to look at the guy on either side of us. They said one of us would not be there six months from then. They were right. Over one-third of our class flunked out.

The class work was not that difficult for me. I had already studied most of the subjects, except for how nuclear reactors worked. The ensign teaching the physics class had a degree in chemistry from Purdue, but his background in physics was from the same class that I had taken while I was at Purdue. I went to sleep in class sometime in the first week. He woke me up, and asked if I thought I would pass his class. I told him we had both taken the same physics class at Purdue, and if he could teach it, I should be able to pass it. His only answer was that I had better pass.

Physics at Purdue is the only class I've ever flunked in my life. I had a class on Saturday mornings that I cut most of the time. They gave a quiz every week that counted as one-third of your grade. Since I never went, I flunked. I got a B in his class, though. I aced the first test, and he got off my ass after that. I admit I wondered to myself why I didn't do as well when I was at Purdue. I don't think of myself as smart, but I usually did well at school if I applied myself. What I lacked was self-discipline. I was a walking example that being a dumbass has nothing to do with intelligence.

Most weekends we'd go into Vallejo or San Francisco. They posted a list of places that were out of bounds (restricted for military). Most of the places on the list were our favorites, so we never went in uniform. I spent my twenty-first birthday in San Francisco. Four of us hit most of the good bars. The bars carded everyone who entered, and when they saw that it was my birthday they gave us our first drinks for free. Most had a two-drink minimum, so we'd drink one more and go to the next bar. By around 3 AM we were all pretty out of it.

The other three all wanted to go back to the base, but naturally I didn't want to go. This is a perfect example of the way my mind worked when I was drunk. I had absolutely no control of what I did. I know I was smart enough to know better, but the alcohol allowed the dumbass side to completely dominate. So I decided staying in San Francisco alone drunk on my ass was no big deal. The other guys knew that there was nothing they could do. They left me sitting on a curb in the middle of San Francisco, and made the hour-long drive back to base. When my roommate got to our room, I was in my bunk asleep. It freaked him out! He woke me up and asked me how I got back. I had no idea. I didn't know I *was* back. No one ever found out how I got there. It was basically a physical impossibility for me to have beaten them back.

That was the first of two episodes in my life I call the "twilight zone" times.

Our main hangout in Vallejo was a pizza place that had live bands and cheap beer. There were always lots of local girls there who liked sailors. The local guys, of course, did not like us. One night, my roommate and I had only been there a few minutes when two guys from our class came looking for us. They had stopped at a liquor store earlier, and five of the locals had jumped them. They wanted us to go with them to find these guys.

Like idiots we went with them. We found the guys in a parking lot close to the liquor store. We got out of the car, and in an instant found ourselves surrounded by fifty or more people, all armed with various weapons. One guy was even swinging a crutch at me. I couldn't believe it!

We fought our way back to the car, but they never stopped attacking. They were hitting the car with everything. The noise was like nothing I'd ever heard before or since.

I was screaming, "Go! Run over them! Just go!"

The car had just started moving when the window on the passenger door exploded in my face. It seemed like forever before we got out of that parking lot. I was picking glass out of my hair, eyes, face, and clothes for a long time. The car was completely totaled. Although we went to the cops, I don't think anything was ever done about it. The locals kept a low profile after that. They knew payback was coming. I heard it arrived later that year after we had left. I was really pissed off I wasn't part of it. I knew I shouldn't have been involved in the first place, but they attacked guys just because they were sailors. At that time I thought they deserved what they got.

During the last few weeks of school, we had to request which of the nuclear prototypes we wanted. A prototype is just a landlocked boat. It is exactly the same as an actual boat, but without the crew quarters. We would spend the next six months there putting our knowledge into practice in an actual nuclear power plant. All together, there were three nuclear prototypes. Two were submarine prototypes: one in Windsor Locks, Connecticut, and the other somewhere in New York. The third prototype was for the only nuclear surface ship at that time, the aircraft carrier USS Enterprise. It was located in Idaho Falls, Idaho. Nobody in my class wanted to go to Idaho. We had heard that it was out in the middle of nowhere, and the daily commute to the plant took about an hour each way by bus. Besides, we were going to submarines.

Scuttlebutt, or gossip, is a normal part of Navy life. I told my roommate that if you tell a lie convincingly enough and often enough, people will believe it even if they don't think it's true. He didn't agree with me, so I told him I would prove it if he helped me. So we started telling everyone that we heard there was a new sub prototype opening in Kansas. The rumor spread through the school like wildfire. It got all the way to the school commander, and he was not amused by it. A lot of people requested Kansas, and others were bitching that they didn't want to go there. The commander had to call a special assembly to stop the rumor! I think I proved my point. Just because everyone believes something doesn't make it true. Later in my life I would use similar examples to teach my martial art students to think for themselves, and not just go along because of peer pressure.

I was slated to go to one of the submarine prototypes, so my choice was between New York and Windsor Locks. I requested the plant in New York. I thought New York would be a more interesting place to live. I told the chief that my future wife lived there. He asked me what she did, and I told him, "I don't know. I haven't met her yet!" Instead, I received orders for the plant in Windsor Locks. Ironically, I did get engaged to a schoolteacher while I was there.

Around that same time, the Navy came to our class with another "deal." If we would extend our enlistment to seven years, we could get a couple of automatic promotions, more money when we started working in a nuclear billet, and a guarantee of our choice for a trade school like air conditioning and refrigeration or compressed gas. We were shown what we'd be making as an E-5 with sub pay and pro pay. It turned out to be a lot of money for that time period. You guessed it. I took them up on the deal. You're not really surprised, are you? At that time I figured I might stay in the Navy if I was on a nuclear sub, and this was a fast track to increase in rank. Of course the pay increase would be nice also. If things had gone the way they were supposed to go, it would have been a good decision. At that time I believed the Navy would live up to their contract. Only a dumbass would make that assumption.

I was immediately promoted to MM3. Since I had more money, I bought my first car. It was a yellow GTO with black interior. It had a 389 engine with a four-speed and competition clutch. It was just what a drunken sailor needs—a car that can reach 130 miles per hour. After graduation, two classmates and I drove it to Connecticut for duty at the prototype. There were no speed limits in the desert. Most of the trip to Hartford was made at speeds over one hundred miles per hour. It's hard to believe we never ran over anyone or got a ticket. Luckily, we managed to make it to Hartford. We found a pretty nice apartment about thirty minutes away from the plant at Windsor Locks.

Rank patch, service medals, and ribbons.

Picture submitted with NAVCAD application.

Boot camp haircut (author on left).

Prototype—Nuclear Hell

T he NPTU (Navy Prototype Training Unit) S1C is in Windsor Locks out in a remote wooded area. It's the prototype of the USS Tullibee (SSN-597), and although the Tullibee is the only exact duplicate, most nuclear submarine power plants are similar. We wore civilian clothes to and from the site. Security was pretty tight, and we were not supposed to talk about anything outside the site. We had picture IDs and were signed in and out by guards. We also had to pass through radiation detectors and got film badges that kept track of our personal radiation exposure.

Like nuclear power school, they told us that one-third or more of our crew would not make it to qualification. Washouts would be sent to the conventional fleet for the term of their enlistment, which was six to seven years. We were divided into three crews. Each crew worked a twelve hour shift. The shifts ran from 8 AM to 8 PM, noon to midnight, and 8 PM to 8 AM. We were given two operation manuals that covered every system in the boat. During a twelve hour shift, we spent eight hours studying the manuals and four hours on watch in the hull. When you were on watch, it was four hours of one emergency after another. Every time you got everything back to normal for a few minutes, something else would go wrong. Each watch station instructor was responsible for training you on that station. If an instructor was out of the hull for more than fourteen days, he had to re-qualify. It was serious shit! You would not sink, but you could cause a nuclear incident. Things had to be done quickly and correctly. It was four hours of stress for everyone, and four hours of hell for me. I was just not getting it. I was pretty sure I would wash out. It was just a matter of how long it would take.

Each system on the boat was assigned a certain number of points. We had to make two hundred points a week. On the eight hours out of the hull, we read the manuals. When we thought we were ready and knew a system, one of the instructors would test us. First we had to draw the system with every valve or switch, with each labeled as normally open or closed. Then the instructor asked questions about abnormal operations. We had to answer immediately and correctly. If we passed, he signed off on our book, and we got the points. If not, we went back to study and had to repeat the process. If we made point count, we got days off before changing shifts. If we missed point count, we had to work our off days with another crew. The second time we missed point count, we did sixteen-hour days—twelve with our crew plus four with the next crew. Miss three times and we had to move onto the site into the "Hymey Hilton" (named after Hyman Rickover—father of the nuclear program). We only had one other choice, which was we could leave. Making point count became harder each week. We ran out of big point systems. I think I made point count the first eight weeks. The tenth week, I went to sixteen hour days, and I was behind on qualifying on watch station.

Although it seemed that I spent all of my time at the plant, there was still time to party. Even though I knew I was drinking too much, it was the only thing that relieved the stress. One night while on the noon to midnight shift, I got off watch and went to study with another crew member. He was a little fat Italian named Tony from New Jersey, and he always found things for us to talk about, like names of movie cowboy's horses, that would break up the study session. That night it was just him and me in the room when we began to study.

All at once he shouted, "God, if there's a God, get me out of here!" Then the lights went out! After a minute or so, he said, "Webster, do you think I pissed him off?" I just laughed and told him I didn't think even God could get us out of there. We sat in the dark discussing this, and pretty soon an officer came around and told us we could leave if our watch was over. The whole East Coast had lost power! We left quickly before he could change his mind. It was really weird going home. There wasn't a light anywhere. Even the stop lights were out so there were traffic jams and wrecks everywhere. We managed to get home and immediately threw a "lights out" party. We invited everyone in the apartment building, and most of them came. There was a lot of booze and candles all over the place. I'm surprised we didn't burn the building down.

That was the night Frank told me his plans for the future. He said as soon as he got to the fleet and was nuclear qualified, he was going to get out of the Navy on a Section 8 discharge for being crazy. Then he would go home and get a job at a civilian nuclear plant near his home, and make big money with the education the Navy had provided. Of course I just laughed at him. Little did I know that he was serious, and that by telling me, he would affect my future. A couple of years later, I heard he had done it and actually got out!

Sometime around the tenth week, I had a problem with one of my roommates, so I moved in with three guys from another crew. They lived over a bar. That cut down on the drunk driving, but made it easier to drink more. I managed to get myself thrown in jail on Christmas Eve. You would think everyone would be in a good mood on Christmas Eve, but any time you've got a bar full of drunks, there's always going to be trouble. I don't remember what happened exactly, but if there was a fight I would usually be involved. They let me out Christmas morning. When they found out I was a sailor they never charged me, but called my crew chief. I did a sixteen hour day with another crew. Happy holidays! It was better than being in jail, but not by much.

I met my future wife, a high school French teacher named Pauline, at a New Year's Eve party, but it didn't turn out exactly as I had imagined. She was with someone from another crew, but I got her number and started spending all of my free time with her. She knew I would probably be stationed out of the States if I got a ballistic sub, but she wanted to travel too. If we were married I would be making pretty good money, and she thought she could find a place to teach part-time if it was necessary. We decided when I got out I could go back and finish school. Things were looking okay, so we got engaged. From that time on, I cut way back on the drinking and spent more time working on qualifying. Time was running out, and the stress was increasing daily. Then we heard some very disturbing scuttlebutt. They were saying that the MMs and BTs in our class were going to the fleet to conventional surface ships, not sub school. I really didn't believe it. The Navy wouldn't waste all that money to train us. Besides, I had a contract. I signed up for submarines. They had to send me to sub school, didn't they?

I completed my point book and got signed off on all the watch stations. It was time for the final oral boards. They had to be done with a different crew. The board consisted of four enlisted instructors and one officer. Mine was scheduled at midnight two days after everything was signed off. When I reported to the board, I found out a guy from another crew would be tested at the same time. They asked me the first question. It was hard, but a reasonable question. Then they asked him one that he couldn't answer, and I wouldn't have been able to answer either. Then they asked me another reasonable question. They asked him something neither of us could answer. That was when we both knew he was not going to qualify. He was black. It pissed me off, but I was busy trying to save my own ass. It continued like that for almost two hours. Then they sent us out of the room to wait for their decision. I thought I had done reasonably well. He and I knew he was finished. We were called back after only twenty minutes. He flunked. He was gone. As for me, they said I had hesitated too long before answering one of the questions. So I would have a partial re-board. It would cover only emergency situations, and they scheduled it for midnight in three days. I could not believe it. The thought of reading those manuals for three more days was more than I could take. I slept little that night. The next day I went on a mission to find out my orders. I knew one of the personnel clerks from a crew party, so I found him and took him to a bar. I found out where I was headed—the USS Markab AR-23. A repair ship, not sub school! I went crazy. I stayed drunk for most of the next three days. I did study some, but I really didn't care. What difference would it make? I was screwed and it was no rumor.

I showed up for my partial board on time at midnight. I was a little drunk, but on time. Everyone was there but the officer. After waiting for fifteen minutes, the chief said they might as well start. It was only supposed to last for an hour. After answering a question from each member of the board quickly and correctly, the chief said they were satisfied and I had passed. Suddenly, this asshole ensign came in carrying both manuals. The chief told him we were done, and he said not yet. He wanted to ask some questions. He opened one of the manuals, and for the next six hours I basically recited both manuals to him. I got one five-minute break because my mouth got so dry that I couldn't talk. I was definitely sober and pissed off, and I wasn't the only one. Everyone in the room wanted to kill that asshole. The chief was sitting behind him, and sometimes he'd mouth the answer to me if I was hesitating.

Around 7:15 AM he asked, "What would happen if we send you out of here to a nuclear submarine?"

"Don't worry about it, because that isn't going to happen!"

"What do you mean by that?"

"Well, the USS Markab might go down, but if it comes back up I'll kiss your ass."

Now he was pissed off. He said, "You're not supposed to know your orders."

"Yeah, that's true," I said. "But it's also true I'm supposed to be going to sub school, so I guess the truth doesn't really matter now, does it? I don't care if you pass me or not," I continued. "Do what you want. I've had enough of this shit and I'm going home." I got up and left the room. It was 7:35 AM.

Later that day I found out they passed me. At that time I also picked up my orders for the USS Markab AR-23, and was sent to the security officer for debriefing. He gave me the easiest order I ever received. He said, "Forget everything we've told you."

"Forget what?" I replied.

As I left the site for the last time, I realized that I wasn't the only one affected by this change of course my life had taken. Since I was engaged, Pauline's life would be affected if she stayed with me. I had no choice, and after the way I had lived my life, I was probably getting what I deserved. I was the dumbass who had quit school and become a drunk. She was a nice person and didn't deserve to be taken down with me. Although I didn't want to do it, I had to break the engagement for her sake. I didn't know how to tell her. Believe it or not, I had actually read about something like this in an Ann Landers column. She had advised the reader to do it in a nice restaurant, and the girl wouldn't make a scene in front of all the people. True to dumbass fashion, I took that advice. When I got back to my apartment she was waiting for me.

"Well, what happened? Did you pass?"

"Believe it or not I passed, and I'm now nuclear qualified. I also got my orders."

"How long do we have before you have to go to sub school? New London's not that far from here. I can come down on weekends."

"I've got to get some sleep. It's been a long night. We'll go out tonight and talk about it."

That night we went to a nice restaurant. We finished eating, and I sat looking at her for a minute or two without saying anything.

"What's wrong? Why are you looking at me like that?"

"I'm not going to sub school."

"I don't understand. What do you mean you're not going to sub school? You said you qualified. Why aren't you going?"

"The Navy says they don't need my rating on the nuclear boats now. I'm going to some piece of crap repair ship somewhere in the Pacific. My life for the next five years is not going to be worth anything to anyone."

"What are you saying? What about us? What about our future?"

"I really can't see that you have a future if you stay with me."

"So you're saying you're breaking up with me? Don't I have a say in this decision?"

"You're young, cute, and educated. You deserve more out of life than I can give you."

She looked at me for a minute, and then started crying loudly. She stood up and very loudly called me several not so nice names, then threw the ring at me and left. I was the center of attention for the whole restaurant. They were all looking at me like hell would be too nice of a place for me to go. I picked up the ring, left money on the table, and went to the bar under my apartment and got drunk. I never said anything to anyone. I thought I had done the right thing, but I did some crying of my own. I know if I ever meet Ann Landers I'm going to kick her ass.

The next day I had just gotten out of bed with a killer hangover when someone started pounding on the door. Every knock made my head feel like it was going to blow up. I yanked the door open ready to punch out whoever dared to be pounding on my door. There she stood. She walked passed me and slammed the door.

"I want my ring back!"

"I don't care if you keep the ring. It's yours. I gave it to you."

"You don't understand. I want you and the ring back. I'm old enough to decide for myself how I want to live my life. We'll make it. I know you'll find a way."

Against my better judgment I gave her back the ring. Maybe with her help I might still have a chance to change things. I promised her I would try. In the back of my mind I still had hope.

Section 8

I had several days before I had to report to the ship. I spent a few days in Hartford saying good-bye to my fiancée, and then I drove to Indiana. I left my car there. I was going to the Pacific Ocean for an undetermined amount of time, so I had little use for a car. I told my father he could drive it, but it was too hot for him. He kept it running for a few months, but it finally wound up sitting in the yard. The next time I would see it, there would be weeds growing up into the engine.

The ship was en route to the Philippines. I was flown on a civilian aircraft leased by the military from California to Clark Air Force Base in the Philippines. It was a very long thirteen-hour flight. I remember getting off the plane in my dress blues, and it was hotter than hell there. I had to take a bus to Manila. The ship was anchored in Manila Bay, and it was the middle of the night when I reported aboard. On the launch going out to the ship, all I could think was that it was definitely not a nuclear submarine or a combat ship. There would be no sub pay, pro pay, or combat pay. I was just a fleet MM3 with more than five long years ahead of me.

Since I was an MM3, there were three places they could put me: the engine room, the outside repair shop, or the valve and pump shop. I was taken to meet the engineering officer. He was a chief warrant officer, and he would decide where I would work. He left me standing at attention for several minutes while he read my service record. Then I got my "welcome aboard" speech, and it was not a morale builder.

He said, "I see you've got two years of college and you're nuclear qualified. You must think you're a smart ass. Well, I don't like a smart ass, and I especially don't like nuclear pukes. We'll see how smart you are. Your ass belongs to me now."

What the hell could I say to that? "Yes sir, thank you sir," I said as I stood there looking at him. I almost said, "Now I know why it took you so long to acknowledge me. You can't read very fast and big words like nuclear are hard for you." I should have said it. The valve and pump shop needed men, so that was where he assigned me. It turned out that was probably the best of the three options. There were around ten men, and I was the third highest rank after the chief and the MM1. There was another MM3, but I had seniority over him. They were a pretty good group, but they were young and only a couple had finished high school.

The engineering office used that fact to jump my ass many times. If anything went wrong on any job, even though I was not in charge, I would get blamed. If the paperwork was not done perfectly, the engineering officer would say "I thought you were a smart college man. Why isn't this done correctly?"

"I was not in charge of that job sir."

"You're the big college man. You should check all of the reports to make sure they're written up right. Maybe you can think about that on the 0400–0800 watch tonight."

So I got volunteered for many night watches, and any other dirty job the officer could think of. He knew I hated the engine room, so anytime they needed help, he'd send me there to give them the benefit of my "superior nuclear knowledge" of engine rooms. He'd go out of his way to make sure I had plenty of extra jobs to keep me busy. I never let him get to me. He was looking for any way he could find to get me busted back in rank. The guys in the valve and pump shop were actually impressed that I had two years of college. During my time with them, I helped them fill out pay chits (similar to checks), tutored them for promotion tests, and did their taxes. They did their jobs and that made it easier for me. I learned a lot from them.

The ship moved to Subic Bay, a Naval base in the Philippines. We remained there most of the time tied up to a pier. The ships coming off the line would tie up next to us, and if they had valve and pump problems, they brought them to us to repair. If the part was too big to remove, the outside repair gang would go to the other ship to do the repairs. Off duty, most of the men went into town every night. They had many stories to tell every day, and they wanted me to go with them. I resisted for a few weeks. I wrote to my fiancée every day and tried to stay away from trouble of any kind. My friendly engineering officer was just waiting for a chance to hang me. My men never gave up easily though. "Webster, we heard you were a hard partying ladies man. Why won't you come to town? You won't believe there's so much booze, and beautiful girls that will do things you've never even imagined. Are you too good to hang out with us lowly high school dropouts?"

"You guys know I'm engaged, and you know our asshole leader is just waiting for an excuse to bust me."

"Yeah, that's a definite fact. But you might as well face it. You've got over five years ahead of you, and you might as well be in jail if all you're going to do is sit on this piece of junk and write letters to a girl you're probably never going to see again. You might see her on a thirty-day leave, but is she going to be happy with that and wait five years for you? Do you think she's going to marry a fleet sailor and live in Olongapo?"

They were right. I was going no place, and it was going to take a long time to get there. I wrote to her and told her we might as well face the facts. We were ten thousand miles apart, and my future wasn't looking too bright. She was a smart girl. She knew any future for us was pretty much doomed. So basically, we both agreed the engagement was over. I told her she could keep the ring, but she sent it back to me. In her last letter she said that she would always wonder what happened to me. Maybe she will read this someday, and know I survived. If things had gone as we had planned, who knows? I hope she's had a happy life. I admit I wonder about her today too.

So they finally talked me into going, and my life took a whole new direction, mostly downhill. I became a real fleet sailor. Olongapo, the town outside the naval base, was like nothing I'd ever seen or even imagined. The population was around one hundred thousand, but the military was only allowed on the main street. It was around two miles long, and there were more than four hundred bars and night clubs lining both sides of the street. Each bar had a band and girls—anywhere from ten to one hundred of them—depending on the size of the bar. Most had a hotel above the bar. There were more than five thousand licensed bar girls. They had to have a weekly physical and be tested for sexually transmitted diseases. There were also street walkers, town girls, and military wives and dependents. It was a sailor's heaven. Every day, from early afternoon until 1 AM curfew, it was one big drunken orgy and brawl. Main Street was bumper-to-bumper with jeep taxis. There were way too many to count. It was always one big, loud traffic jam, especially at the curfew when everyone was heading back to the base. The base was separated from the city by a river spanned by a fairly long bridge. I still dream about crossing that bridge over "Shit River" going into "Po City."

The other MM3 in the shop was a Mexican named Ramone, and he was my primary drinking partner. We had a lot of amazing adventures, but the best one happened when the ship went to Hong Kong. A few months before we went to Hong Kong we got a new man in the shop. He was an eighteen-year-old nerd type named Fultz. His father owned a trucking company. I think he joined the Navy to get away from his father. He was definitely not the truck driver type of guy. He was really a weird kid. Of course he was the target of many jokes, like most new guys.

"Hey Fultz, have you ever had a girlfriend?"

"Yeah I've had a girlfriend. You think I'm queer or something?"

"Got a picture of her naked?"

"No!"

"Want to buy one?"

"What the hell are you guys talking about?"

I don't think he'd ever drunk a beer or kissed a girl. He wouldn't go into Olongapo with us, but he'd go to the base store and buy lots of expensive things. I think his father sent him money pretty often. One day the chief noticed something else odd about him. If there was even the slightest defect on whatever he bought he didn't want it anymore. So if he bought something the chief liked (I remember a nice stereo system), the chief would soon own it. He's put a scratch on it. Then it went something like this.

"Hey Fultz, that's a nice stereo. Where'd you get it?"

"It was on sale at the base store."

"What'd it cost you?"

"It was only three hundred dollars."

"I guess it was on sale because of this scratch on it."

"What scratch? Damn it. I never saw that. Shit."

"It's not that big. It won't bother the way it plays."

"Shit. I'm going to take it back. I don't want it if it's scratched."

"I hate to tell you this Fultz. They won't take it back if it was on sale."

"Shit! Shit! Shit!"

"Tell you what Fultz. I really don't like the scratch, but I'll give you a $100 for it."

"Do you mean it chief? Thanks. I really appreciate it. It's yours."

So the chief got a nice stereo cheap. I felt sorry for Fultz. I tried to explain to him what the chief was doing, but he wouldn't believe me. I couldn't believe anyone could be that dumb, but finally I gave up trying to help him. I didn't know then that he'd play a big part in my Hong Kong adventure.

The first day in Hong Kong my buddy Ramone and I got pretty drunk by noon. Hong Kong is another sailor's paradise. Chinese women are prettier to me than Filipino women, and they got even more appealing the more we drank. We left a bar and got into a couple of rickshaws. The men pulling them were old and skinny, but boy could they run! We had them race and I'm surprised they didn't keel over. After a few blocks we got out, and a guy on the street asked us if we wanted to go to a "skivvy house" or a whorehouse. Being drunk and stupid, we got in a taxi with this guy.

After driving for twenty minutes or so, I began to think we would never be seen again. We'd been in some rough places, but we were way out of bounds and definitely outnumbered. Finally, the taxi pulled into a long alley and we got out. The guy went to a steel door and knocked. Someone said something from inside, he answered, and the door opened. All this time I'm thinking to myself that we are not going to make it out of here alive. We got into a freight elevator and went up three floors. He knocked on another door and it opened. Sure enough, he had brought us to a skivvy house. There were seven or eight young, cute girls.

We were sitting on a couch drinking beer as we decided which girl to pick when we heard someone clumping down the hallway. Around the corner came Fultz. He had his arm around a girl and a big smile on his face. He saw us and said, "Guess what guys, I ate her!" I almost choked on my beer. We could not stop laughing. We told the pimp that we'd pass on the girls because the mood had been broken. This pissed him off, so we agreed to let him take us to a different place. I made Fultz come with us. I just could not believe he had come out there by himself.

We went a couple of blocks to another building. It was nicer and we went up an elevator to the tenth floor. There was only one girl, and she wasn't that great. We both said no way and the pimp went crazy. He was jumping up and down, screaming and spitting at us. I grabbed the guys and said that we had to leave now or we were going to die there. I didn't have to understand Chinese to know that he was pissed and was yelling for others to join him.

We ran down the stairs while several people chased us. They were yelling and throwing anything they could find: bottles, shoes, anything and everything. We were all laughing like idiots, and even though I was sure we were going to die, I thought it was funny as hell. By the time we got to the street, there were at least fifteen people chasing us. We ran like hell for a couple of blocks with the gang chasing us growing larger. I saw a taxi coming down the street. When it was near us, I jumped in front of it. I had my hand full of Hong Kong money and waved it at the driver. He stopped, and we jumped in, throwing the money at him. All of us screamed "Go, go, go!" He took off like a bat out of hell. I don't know how much I gave the driver, but it must have been enough. I'm sure he remembered the crazy Americans for a long time after that. As for Fultz, he had one hell of a first liberty. For my buddy and me it was a great sea story. We had no idea that even wilder adventures were in store for us.

By the time the ship returned to Subic Bay, my time in grade MM3 was up. I was due for a promotion to MM2 which was one of the conditions guaranteed in my extension for seven years. Big surprise! The engineering officer said he wasn't going to give it to me. I told him I'd contact the chief of naval operations to see what he thought about a chief warrant officer disagreeing with Navy reenlistment policy. It really burned his ass, but he finally gave it to me. He really didn't have a choice at that point. As for the other condition, compressed gas school, he *could* stop that. There was no specified time and I had over four years left. Every day I put in a request, and every day he disapproved it. Finally, he ordered me to stop requesting the school. So every day I requested something different: sub school, any combat ship, anything anywhere! I was then ordered to stop requesting anything.

Around this time Badillio's enlistment was nearing the end. All he talked about was that he was going to be home with a *life*. He planned to be a border patrol officer. He never let me forget my future was to be on the USS Markab forever. The night before he left we went to Olongapo and got really drunk. After we got back to the ship around 2 AM, we were sitting in a loading bay in our underwear and shower shoes still talking about my lack of a future.

He pointed to a tie up rope on the ship and said, "You want out? Climb down that rope and take off across the shipyard. I guarantee you'll get out."

My drunken mind at that time told me that he was right. So I said "Fuck it," and went down the rope and across the shipyard.

Both the quarterdeck watches saw me at the same time. They were yelling "Stop! What the hell are you doing?"

I actually heard the chief on watch say "Shoot him." Shoot me? What the hell was he thinking? Why would you shoot someone who was just walking across a shipyard in his skivvies and shower shoes? The problem was that *I* wasn't sure what I was doing! All I could think to do was continue across the shipyard and try to figure out what to do.

Watson, the MM2 on watch, was a friend from nuclear prototype. He caught up to me easily. I was walking slowly, and I'd lost one of the shower shoes going down the rope.

"Webster, what the fuck are you doing?"

"Hell, I don't know. Did that idiot chief tell you to shoot me?"

Watson laughed. "He sure as hell did. I'd probably be doing you a favor if I did. What's going on? This is weird—even for you."

"Do you remember that fat little Italian who said he was going to get out on a Section 8?"

"Yeah, I can't remember his name, but I remember him talking about it when he was drunk."

"I heard he actually did it. Did you ever hear that?"

"Yeah, but I don't know if it's true or not. Is that what you're doing?"

"I don't know, but it's the only thing I can think of right now. I know I'm definitely screwed if I don't think of something quick."

About that time we were passing a ship in a dry dock. An idea popped into my drunken head. I started walking up a gang plank to the ship. When we were about halfway up, I turned around and saw the chief and some others running our way. Watson was right beside me, and it was a long drop to the bottom of the dry dock. I told him to grab my arm and hold tight.

"What the hell are you doing?"

"Just don't let go and maybe I can get out of this. Hold tight damn it!"

As soon as the others were close, I yelled that I wanted to die, and acted like I was trying to jump into the dry dock. If Watson had let go, I would have been dead. They took me back to the ship and threw me into the brig. I didn't like the guy they made guard me, so I fucked with him most of the night. I'd laugh, cry, rant, and rave. The laughing was real. The look on his face was funny as hell. He actually believed I was crazy. I was so good I thought I was crazy!

When morning came and I sobered up, I realized how bad I had screwed up. There was only one choice for me. I had to carry through with what I'd started. They took me to see the ship's doctor. He had reported aboard only a couple of days earlier. This was his first duty station, and it was going to be an interesting start for his career. He told me to sit down, and he took a chair a few feet in front of me.

Before he said anything, I pulled my chair right up to where our knees were almost touching. I leaned towards him and whispered, "Are you a doctor?"

"Yes I am," he replied softly. All the time I was looking around the room—behind me and to my sides—like I thought someone was slipping up on me. I asked if he went to school, and he very softly and seriously again replied that he had. It was all I could do to keep a straight face.

I said, "You and I are the only ones on this ship who are sane. The rest are idiots—*especially* the engineering officer! I'm sure he wants to kill me!" Our talk continued like this for a few minutes. I'm glad it didn't go longer, because I was having trouble keeping up the act.

A corpsman I knew was standing behind the doctor. He was trying his best not to laugh. When the doctor turned his head once, I winked at the corpsman and he almost lost it. The doctor bought it! I was a very happy, crazy person. They transferred me off the ship to the hospital to see a shrink. When I got to the hospital, I was told the doctor had just left for a thirty-day leave, so they would have to check me into the base transient barracks. Transient is where military personnel stay until they have transportation to their next duty station. Since I was technically in the hospital, the transient office never kept track of me. I wasn't assigned any duties. It was just a place for me to sleep. I had it made! I took the bus to the hospital everyday. I had to be there from 8 AM until 4 PM. Then I would return to the transient barracks and go into town every night. All I did at the hospital was watch television and movies, play pool, and eat pretty good food. The ship had gone back to the states. It was a pretty good month. I know it might seem weird to you, but in over two years in the military, becoming a psychiatric patient was the best duty I had. I met a second class engineman named Jake who was recovering from his second Purple Heart. He was from the "PBRs" (Patrol Boat, River) that patrolled the rivers in Vietnam. Returning from a mission, he had thrown a tie-up rope to a Vietnamese who threw back a grenade. He was mostly recovered and went to town with me several nights.

The doctor finally returned from leave, and I was his first patient. He was a full commander and seemed like a really nice guy. To tell the truth, I was tired of playing crazy. I was off the Markab, and I didn't believe I'd ever see that ship again. So I decided to tell him the truth about everything that had happened to me in the Navy.

"Why are you here? You don't seem to be the person I read about in the incident report."

"It's a long story, but I'll try to tell you a condensed version. Maybe you'll be able to tell me how I went from being a fighter pilot to the lunatic in that report."

"What do you mean about being a fighter pilot?"

"That's the reason I joined the Navy. The Navy had a new program where you could be accepted into flight school without having a degree. If you could pass all the tests, all you needed were two years of college."

"Did you pass all of the tests?"

"I passed all the written tests, the physical and mental tests, and an officer review board."

"It says here that you're nuclear qualified. What's that got to do with flight school?"

"When I was in boot camp they wanted people to go into nuclear power because they needed qualified men on all of the new nuclear submarines they were building. It required a six-year enlistment and being able to make it through nuclear power school, qualification, and sub school."

"I still don't see how that relates to being a pilot."

"It doesn't. They convinced me by saying that I had to commit to six years for the NAVCAD program anyway, and I would still be given that chance. The bait was that I could get out of boot camp in only five weeks, and I could get to flight school quicker."

"What happened to flight school?"

"When I was at MM school, they checked my eyes again. With my pupils dilated, my right eye was not a perfect 20/20. I could not fly fighters. I could only have flown helicopters, so I had to decide between that or a nuclear submarine. I chose wrong, and I also extended my enlistment to seven years for rank promotions and more money when I got to the nuclear submarine."

"You're nuclear qualified. Why aren't you on a nuclear submarine?"

"After spending one hundred thousand dollars (according to them) and putting me through the hell of qualifying, they said they didn't need my rate on the nuclear subs, so they sent me to a repair ship instead of sub school. There I was just another sailor and under the thumb of an idiot warrant officer. He told me he hated me because I went to college and nuclear power school. He tried to stop my rank promotion, and refused to send me to the school I was promised in the enlistment extension. So since the Navy didn't keep the contract with me, I've lost my future, my fiancé, and if I continue being the drunken, fighting sailor I am now, I will have lost what's left of my mind. So, I think I'd be better off with a Section 8 discharge. After telling you all of this, I can't believe that I'm not crazy."

"Well, I certainly understand your anger and disappointment. I know the military does illogical things, and this is amazing even to me. You go have lunch. I want to think about this and talk with another doctor. We'll talk again this afternoon."

When I returned, both doctors were waiting for me. The new one, who was another full commander, stood and shook hands with me, which surprised me. They told me they were sorry I'd had such a bad experience in the Navy, and that they hoped their recommendation would be followed.

They had written a one and a half page evaluation that was going into my service record. They gave me a copy to read, and I was sure it was going to say I should be given a Section 8 discharge. I read it, and I reread it. I could not believe what I was reading! Basically, it said that they were impressed with me, and that the Navy was not utilizing my potential. Their recommendation was that I should be sent to OCS (Officer Candidate School). I was totally speechless. I had tried to get out of the Navy because I was crazy, and now I was being recommended to be an officer! They gave me my service records and said I was released to return to my duty station. They shook my hand and wished me luck. I said, "Thank you, sirs," when I was really thinking, "What in the hell are you crazy assholes thinking?" Did they really think that I was going to return to the Markab and be sent to OCS? I decided then and there that I wasn't crazy enough to be an officer.

I was sitting on a bench waiting for the bus to transient when Jake sat down beside me. He too had just been discharged from the hospital. I let him read what they had written, and he laughed his ass off.

"So, now what are you going to do?"

"I don't know, but I seriously doubt I'll be going to OCS."

"Well, I've only got about six months left on my enlistment. I've got a friend working in the transient office. We have a plan worked out that you might find interesting."

So we went to the transient office and gave his friend our records, and he hid them in some sort of obscure file. I was free! Transient thought I was in the hospital. The hospital thought I was in transient back to the ship. The ship didn't know or care where I was. We left our uniforms at our lockers in the transient barracks, changed into civilian clothes, and went out and rented a house in Olongapo. It was really a weird feeling. I really didn't believe I could just walk away. I knew sooner or later it was going to come back to bite me on the ass, but at that moment I couldn't have cared less. The adventure was only then just beginning.

Po City

The house we rented was pretty big and reasonably nice compared to others in Olongapo. I really can't remember what it cost us. The exchange rate at that time was eight pesos to the dollar, so we were rich compared to our neighbors. We had a lot of girls who cooked, cleaned, did our laundry, and anything else we asked of them. The problem was that the military was confined to the main street, and our house was a long way from there. We had to worry about the military police, Olongapo cops, security cops, and the local gangs. The military police would arrest us, and the others would kill us. Everyone carried weapons of some kind, and none of them would hesitate to use them.

Fortunately, all but the military police could be bought off, and the kids in the neighborhood would warn us if the military or security police were around. There were still too many times that I found myself at the wrong end of a gun explaining what I was doing in that part of town. It cost me several pesos and two or three wristwatches (and they didn't like Timex). Every time I went back on the base, I'd have to replace several things that I'd given away as gifts or bribes.

Each week one of us would go to the transient office, get our pay records from our friend, and go to the base payroll office and get paid. Since we were both E-5, we were making about the same amount. Whoever got paid just split it 50/50 with the other one. We'd take the pay record back to the clerk and he'd file it away. Worked like a charm.

It's almost impossible to describe what my life was like then. Basically, every day we did the same things: drink, dance, fight, and fuck. We decided to try to drink a beer and have a girl in every bar in Olongapo. We were never totally sober, just in different stages of being drunk. On the days we went back on base to get paid, it was a kind of vacation from the partying. We'd go to the base pool, sometimes watch a movie, eat at the Enlisted Men's (EM) club, check our gear at the transient barracks, restock on items at the base store, and then it was back to the animal life. Those days were the only ones that marked time for us. Every other day was a copy of the one before.

On one of those paydays, we met eight Navy "Seabees" (construction engineers) at the EM club. I can't remember exactly what happened, but for some reason they wound up there on their way back to Vietnam. They were having trouble getting a flight because they were in their greens and had their weapons. They were checked into transient, and told to check every day at the air base until they caught a flight. One of them, a chief, had just reenlisted in Vietnam. He had gotten a ten thousand dollar bonus tax free, so they were looking for some I & I (Intoxication & Intercourse).

We invited them to stay at our house. They gladly accepted, and the party went up a few levels, fueled by the chief's bonus money. Still, one of them had to go check at the air base every morning. One morning I went with the chief when he checked. On the way back, we had an interesting moment on the bridge. There were always kids on the bridge wanting to shine your shoes. Sometimes they'd put a glob of polish on your shoe, then you would have to let them shine it off. A boy I guessed was about eight years old tried it on the chief. The chief didn't speak a word. He just reached down, grabbed the kid's ankle, and flung him over the bridge railing about thirty feet out into the river. The kid never had a chance to say anything. He was wide eyed and screaming something as he made several flips before hitting the river with a big splash.

"I guess you don't want your shoes shined," I said.

"Nope," he said, and we continued on our way. After that none of the other kids came near us. Wonder why?

The Seabees finally got a flight back to 'Nam, and I really missed them. One of them gave me a set of his greens. He said maybe they'd bring me luck. He had survived a lot of close calls. Even though I can't remember any of their names, I can still see them clearly in my mind. Actually, I'm glad I can't remember their names. This way I can believe they all made it and their names aren't on that black wall somewhere.

Sometime around the seventh or eighth week, I was sitting in the EM club having a drink after being paid. Suddenly, I felt a lot of pain in my left leg below the knee. I looked at my leg, and it was swollen to about three times its normal size. I was wearing tight jeans, and they were stretched so tight that I couldn't lift my pant leg. I had no idea what was happening. There was a first class corpsman sitting a couple of tables from me, so I decided to ask him to take a look at it.

"Hey doc, I hate to bother you when you're off duty, but could you take a look at my leg?"

He came over and looked at it and his eyes got wide.

"What happened to you?"

"Hell I don't know. I've just been sitting here a couple of hours drinking, and my leg started hurting."

"Can you walk on it?"

I got up and tried to walk, but I couldn't put my weight on that leg. I hobbled back to my chair and sat down.

"You've got to go to the hospital. I'm going to call an ambulance."

"Is that really necessary, doc? Can't you do anything?" I didn't know how I was going to explain my situation to the hospital. He insisted I needed to go and called the ambulance.

Everyone kept asking me what happened, and to be honest, I really didn't know! At the hospital the corpsman split my pant leg and packed my leg in ice. He told me to tell him when it became numb, and then he left the room. I promptly went to sleep, or more accurately, I passed out. When he came back, the swelling had gone down, but my leg was blue. He asked me what ship I was from, and all I told him was that

I was in transient back to the U.S. He then wrote a report and gave it to me for my medical record. He got me a ride back to the transient barracks. I got another pair of pants from my locker and limped back to the house. As soon as I entered the house a couple of my buddies started firing questions at me.

"Where the hell have you been? The other guys are out looking for you."

"I just came from the hospital. Do you guys know what happened to my leg?"

"You don't remember? Come on, nobody could be that drunk. You got run over by a taxi!"

"I really got run over?"

"Hell yes, it knocked you down. Then you got up and started jumping up and down on the hood. We had to pull you away before the shore patrol came or we all would have been screwed. When we got you back here, you passed out on the couch. When we got up this morning you were gone, and we've been looking for you ever since. We thought the shore patrol or the Olongapo police had you. You don't remember any of it?"

"Honest to God. I don't remember anything. Look at my leg!" It was turning many different colors from the knee down. It hurt like hell, but I continued to walk on it. It took three or four weeks for it to start looking normal again. I threw away the report the hospital had given me. I watched where I was walking from then on.

After about three months, I was ready to go back to the U.S. I had almost been caught or killed several times. I told Jake and he understood. He only had a couple of months left on his enlistment, and he was going back pretty soon as well. A couple of nights later, I got caught. I had a girlfriend there and she owned a restaurant. I was hanging out in the restaurant and lost track of time. I couldn't get home before curfew so I decided to sleep in the kitchen. I had just fallen asleep when one of the kitchen boys woke me up yelling, "Shore patrol is coming!" I ran out the back door and stepped on a sleeping pig. He let out a loud squeal! Both of us were scared shitless. I went down and the pig ran off. The pig escaped but the shore patrol caught me.

I knew I was screwed. There was no way I was going to explain why I was sleeping in that kitchen. To make matters worse, I was wearing the greens the Seabee had given me. The shore patrol could not make any sense of it. What was a Navy PO2 doing wearing jungle greens and sleeping in a restaurant in Olongapo? Because I wouldn't tell them anything, they took me to the Marine sergeant on duty. I knew what I had to do. I had to lie my ass off. The Marine was wearing his ribbons. Since one of them was a Bronze Star, and another was a Purple Heart, I knew he had seen plenty of action. So I started talking. I would tell the truth and nothing but the truth. At least most of what I told him had happened was the truth. It just hadn't happened to *me*.

"Listen Gunny, I just got released from the hospital here a couple of days ago. I'm a second class engineman from the PBRs in 'Nam. One night a month or so ago we got a call that some Marines needed some fire support and wounded evacuated. We got them out, but I got hit in my left leg. I got my second Purple Heart while I was in the hospital here. I'm in greens because that's all I had when I came here. I didn't waste my breath on the shore patrol because all they do is bust drunks. I need to get back to my boat. I can tell from your ribbons that you've been there. You understand why I have to get back. If I don't, some other Marines may pay the price." So far he hadn't said a word, but I was watching his face and I could tell I might be getting through to him. So I kept talking.

"I've got a flight back tomorrow. I need to be on it. I'm sure you're not happy doing this duty. Marines are made to fight. I may be in the Navy, but I'm a Marine at heart. All I did was got caught drunk and out after curfew. If you let them bust me I'll miss that flight. All you have to do is tear up that report, and I can get back to the war where I'm needed."

"You've got a flight back tomorrow?"

"The flight's at 0900. If I miss it, I'll be in the shit for that, and who knows when I'll be able to get another one."

"If you're shitting me, you're damn good at it. If I ever see you on this base after tomorrow, you'll know what it's really like to be in the shit."

"Gunny, I promise you that you'll never see me here again. Maybe we'll meet under different circumstances if you ever get back to the war." Then he tore up the report and had another Marine give me a ride to the transient barracks. I couldn't believe I'd talked my way out of another mess. The Seabee had been right. His greens had brought me unbelievable luck.

The next morning I told the clerk to put my records in the right file. The next day I asked the chief at transient when I was going back to the U.S. He asked how long I'd been there. "About three months," I said. I thought he was going to have a heart attack.

"Why have you been here so long?" he asked.

"How the hell should I know? You're the one in charge here," I replied. Three days later, I was on a flight back to California. I was still amazed that I'd gotten away with it. I figured Po City would only be a distant memory. Of course, I was wrong as usual.

Po City bar. (Author fourth from left.)

Section 8—Part Two

By the time I got back to the U.S., the Markab was in San Diego for sea trials getting ready to return to the West Pacific. You can imagine how happy they were to see me again. The look on the engineering officer's face as he read the doctor's report was definitely a Kodak moment. When he finished reading, he just glared at me for a minute or so.

"I really thought I was rid of your smart ass."

"Well sir, I assure you that I gave it my best shot to never lay eyes on this ship or you ever again. I know the Navy is screwed up, but sending me back here is still hard for me to believe. Maybe they knew how much you would miss me, sir."

"Keep it up, smart ass. How you managed to do all of this shit and keep your stripes I'll never understand. In any case, you're my problem again. I promise you that your luck has run out. You can't fool me like you have everyone else."

"Yes sir. I expect it to be interesting. May I point out one thing to you?"

"What are you talking about?"

"In case you missed it, I wanted you to notice that they recommended I become an officer—not a warrant officer. I just wanted to make sure you hadn't missed that."

His face got so red I thought he was going to have a stroke. He didn't really say much else. He told me to report to the chief in the outside repair shop. It really didn't matter to me where he put me. I was already thinking about how to get off again. The next day I started putting in my daily requests for transfer.

The guys in outside repair were okay. Most of them were old drinking buddies, and they couldn't wait to hear about my past few months. The people who knew me thought I was really cool. The others thought I was definitely crazy and gave me plenty of space.

The engineering officer had more problems to worry about. The ship could not pass the sea trials. It was an old piece of shit ship. Every day something else broke down and we had to be towed back into port. The captain was catching hell about it, and he was all over the engineering officer's ass to get everything up and running. Meanwhile, there was an MM2 on a cruiser who was willing to trade duties with me. He didn't like the long combat missions, and thought a ship that stayed tied up at the dock was a good thing.

One night I went to his ship to check it out. I agreed to trade if he could arrange it. So we went to a bar in San Diego to plan the best way to make the switch. After we worked it out, I headed back to the ship in a pretty good mood.

The liberty boat back to the ship was full of drunks as usual. I was talking to another MM2 and minding my own business when one of the other guys came up and butted in on our conversation.

"I've heard about you. You don't look so tough to me."

"You're right. I'm not as tough as they say I am. Now that you've made me admit that, you go tell your friends how you scared me."

He pushed me and went back to his friends, but he kept mouthing off. On board, he followed me all the way down to my bunk. The more I ignored him, the bolder he became. The whole time he kept telling me what a badass he was, and that he wasn't afraid of me.

I took off my uniform and put it on my bunk. He was still there.

"I'm telling you one last time to walk away from me."

He came at me, and I knocked him on his bad ass. He hit the deck, then got up and took off running. After all his talk, this really pissed me off, so I chased him. He was running like hell and yelling for someone to help him. He ran into a shop where a poker game was going on, and they stopped me and convinced me to let things go. Can you picture this in your mind? Here's this crazy guy in his underwear, chasing some poor innocent guy around the ship trying to kill him. Guess who was off the ship the next morning?

The next morning, two guys from shore patrol had me pack my sea bag, gave me my records, and drove me to the locked ward at the base hospital. It was on the Friday before Labor Day, and of course all of the doctors were going to be gone for the holiday weekend. It was a long three days. There were ten or so other guys in the ward, and one guy was locked in a padded room yelling as loud as he could.

My mind raced. "I think I've seen this movie before. Damn, I'm Jack Nicholson in *One Flew Over The Cuckoo's Nest*. Are these guys as crazy as they seem, or are they doing the same thing I'm doing? What the hell am I doing? Am I acting, or am I really crazy?" I'll admit I didn't know myself anymore. I tried to stay away from the other guys. I spent most of my time reading or talking to the corpsman on duty. On Tuesday morning, I got to see a doctor. He asked me what had happened. I told him to read it for himself, because if I told him the story, he wouldn't believe it. He read for quite a while.

Then shook his head and said, "You're right, it's unbelievable. I can tell you that you've been incredibly lucky. I'm surprised you're still alive. I can't give you a Section 8, but I'll tell you that you better stay away from the booze. You're off that ship now. You've got over four years ahead of you. You're smart enough to be a good sailor, but if you keep drinking you're not going to make it. Face the facts, and stop drinking."

He discharged me, and I went to the transient barracks in San Diego to wait for new orders. The Markab had left for the West Pacific a couple of days earlier. I wondered if they'd make it without breaking down. The fact that it was gone put me in a really good mood. I had to laugh when I thought about how my legend would grow now. The guys on that ship had a great new sea story to tell.

Transient Troubles

My time spent in transient in San Diego was pretty easy duty. Some mornings I'd have to do chores like supervise some work parties cleaning the barracks. I also had to do some shore patrol rotations. It seemed funny to be the one doing the arresting. It was pretty easy most of the time. Someone had to be really out of control for me to take them to jail. Mostly we just took them back to the ships.

Of course, I still got picked up by the shore patrol. It seemed I spent most of my time arresting people or being arrested. What a life. I'd start drinking in the early afternoon, and by nighttime I was usually bombed out of my mind. One night I lost my hat at a bar, so I got picked up because I was out of uniform and drunk. They kept me locked up for four hours until I sobered up some, and then they let me go. During that time I remembered where my hat was. Some guy in a bar had taken it. I decided I was going to go back and get it. I had to take him on with his friends. This led to my second arrest for the night but I did get my hat back! Since that was my second arrest in six hours, they kept me all night. They sent a report to the transient officer. All he did was confine me to the barracks. Big deal!

One morning I was called to the transient office. I figured I'd gotten new orders. I knew I hadn't been in any trouble recently. I reported to the transient officer.

"I'm sorry to have to tell you this, but your mother has had a heart attack. She's in pretty bad shape. I'm going to authorize ten days emergency leave for you."

"Sir, I don't have any money to go home. I haven't been paid for quite a while. I'm not even sure where my pay records are."

"Check with the Red Cross. They'll loan you the money. You can pay them back when you get back. I'll make sure to find your pay records by then."

So I went to the Red Cross office on base, and they loaned me the money for a plane ticket and traveling money. They also arranged a ride to the airport for me. On the plane home, I realized I hadn't even talked to my parents in quite a while. They still didn't have a telephone, and I hadn't written a letter to anyone in a long time. It's hard to describe my emotional state. The life I'd been living had pretty much destroyed my normal thinking process. I realized I'd been living day-to-day like a robot, pretty much devoid of any emotions. I wondered how the Navy tracked me down. Hell, even I wasn't sure where I was most of the time.

By the time I got home, my mother had pulled through and was going to make it. She was going to be in the hospital for a few days to stabilize before they sent her home. When I wasn't at the hospital, I got the GTO running again and sold it to my buddy James. I had no use for a car. I could use the money to pay back the Red Cross. The day before they were going to discharge my mother, I spent most of the afternoon drinking with some old friends. I was drunk as usual when I went home. We had some new neighbors I didn't know, and I ended up getting into a dispute with them. I really can't remember why. The argument didn't become physical, but I was really pissed. Not only had I not stopped drinking, I had turned into an aggressive drunk who wanted to destroy anything or anyone around me. I went through the back door of our house and into the kitchen. A cabinet door was standing open, and I punched it. It exploded and shattered into pieces! That really set me off. My dad tried to reason with me, but he was no match for a veteran bar fighter. I started punching and kicking everything in sight. I continued through the house kicking, punching, and turning over furniture, until I went out the front door without opening it. The house had taken all of the aggression out of me. Destroying the house was bad, but it was better the house than the neighbors. I was standing on the front porch when a police car pulled into the driveway. The neighbors had called them.

I knew the cop. I had known him all my life. He lived a couple of blocks from there, and I used to hang out with his younger brother. When he walked up steps, I just sat down.

"Mike, what's going on? Did you do all of this? Are you alright?"

"No, Ron, I wouldn't say I was alright. Look at what I've done. Would you say that anyone who could do that would be alright? I'm a drunk and I'm dangerous. Just take me to jail. That's where I belong." I walked down to the police car and got in the back seat. Ron walked through the house and talked to my dad for awhile. Then he came and took me to jail. We didn't speak. The county jail was about half a block from my dad's barber shop. The next morning the sheriff, who also had known me all my life, came and let me out.

"Well, Mike, it seems you had quite a night. What's happened to you? I thought you were in school at Purdue."

"That seems like a thousand years ago. Obviously that person is long gone."

"I talked to your dad. He doesn't understand this anymore than I do. He doesn't want to press any charges. What are you going to do if I let you go?"

"I'm supposed to bring my mother home from the hospital. I guess that'll be later today after the house is repaired. As soon as I do that, I'll leave for California."

"I'm going to let you go. I still find it hard to believe you've changed so much. In any case, I want you gone today, or I'll forget old times and charge you myself. Do you understand?"

That afternoon, I had to go get my mother, explain why she had to wait most of the day for me to come get her, and why her house was pretty much destroyed. I felt lower than whale shit. After I got her home and settled, I started packing. My dad came to talk to me.

"Why are you leaving today? You've still got three days left on your leave."

"Don't you think I've done enough damage? Besides, the sheriff told me to leave town."

"He didn't mean you had to leave today."

"Believe me, he means today. I've told both you and mom I'm sorry, but I know you'll never understand. I left enough money to pay for the repairs. I can't explain it. Sorry."

So then I left for California. I had been run out of my hometown before sundown. I was really a son to be proud of. Only a real dumbass would not change after that.

The day after I got back to transient, I received my new orders. I sat down on the steps outside the office to read them. I was to report to the USS Markab! I sat there for a long time trying to make some sense out of the order. This was way beyond unbelievable. I went back into the office and demanded to see the transient officer. I told him I couldn't believe even the Navy could be that stupid. I told him to read my records. I had been thrown off that ship twice.

"That ship doesn't want me back, and I can guarantee that I won't go back. Either you get me any other ship in the combat zone, or lock my ass up in the brig. I will not return to that ship!" I said.

He told me to come back in a couple of hours. I got new orders. I was to report to the USS Passumpsic AO-107. It was a supertanker, and was in Long Beach preparing to deploy to Vietnam.

Check Your Oil?

I t should be obvious that a floating gas station would not be my first choice of duty. However, it was a step up from a repair ship. At least this ship would not stay tied to a pier, and it would get me into the combat zone. I might be able to get someone there to help me get where I wanted to be. At that time I really didn't have a plan except to stay out of trouble. Of course it never worked out like that.

Things started out okay at first. When I reported aboard the Passumpsic, my reception was totally opposite the one I had on the Markab. Again the division officer was a CWO4, but this one liked me from the start. They didn't need an MM2 in the engine room, so I was put in charge of "Happy Valley." That was what they called the pump room on the ship. It contained the main feed pumps and bilge pumps, and it was under the boiler room. "Hell's Basement" would have been a better name for it. My boss was a BT (Boiler Tender) chief, and I had a BT3 and two firemen under me. The chief wasn't pleased to have an MM2 instead of a BT working for him, but we got along until my dark side caught up to me.

I had only been aboard about three weeks when I got into trouble again. I hadn't been off the ship since I reported aboard, and one of the MM3s from the engine room talked me into going into town with him. Of course he meant to a bar. I knew better, but that's what sailors do. We got into a fight with some civilians in a Long Beach bar. We got locked up, and it was almost noon the next day when the shore patrol returned us to the ship. I was changing clothes when the chief found me.

"Where the hell have you been?" He was red-faced and yelling at the top of his lungs. I started to say something, but he never let me get a word out.

"One of your men is probably dead. I don't care what your excuse is, this fucking off has gotten a man killed, and I'm going to make sure your ass pays for it."

Then he turned around and left. He was still muttering and cussing to himself. He never said who or what had happened. I was left standing there with my mouth hanging open trying to make some sense out of what he'd said. I found out what had happened from one of the BTs. One of the main feed pumps had broken down, and to work on it the men had to lift it off the deck. It got away from them and fell on one of the fireman. He happened to be a good kid I really liked. He wasn't dead, but his back was broken. I spent the rest of that day in a kind of shock. I sat out on the deck thinking about it. The guilt I felt was overwhelming. I had screwed up again, and someone else had paid for it. The chief was right. I should have been there. However, it turned out that he wasn't there either, and he should have been. He knew I wasn't there, so he should have been supervising them. That was the main reason he hung everything on me. He knew he was guilty too. He gave it his best shot. I was sent to captain's mast within the week.

I know it's hard to believe, but with all the shit I'd pulled, this was the first time I was ever put on report. There went my good conduct medal. At the captain's mast, the other men reported what had happened. I don't remember the specific charges, but when the chief finished talking there was no doubt he thought I should hang, and he'd be happy to buy the rope. Then the captain asked me to respond. How could I respond to this?

Like the time with the hospital doctors, I decided to tell the truth. I told him that everything that had been said was true. I said, "I know you've read my records, so you know how I wound up on your ship. I don't know if anything different would have happened if I'd been there, but I should have been there. The chief knew I wasn't there, so he should have been there. He can delegate authority, but he can't delegate responsibility. He was yelling that one of 'my' men was dead. Wasn't the kid one of his men too? I have no excuse. I am guilty, and I know I've got to live the rest of my life knowing it. I don't know about the chief, but I'm never going to sleep good again. I liked that kid." I only got five days restriction and a twenty-five dollar fine. I also got a lifetime of guilt.

Needless to say, the chief was not happy with the captain's decision. I admit I was surprised at such a lenient punishment. It proved my theory that the whole world was crazy. Restricted men had to muster five times a day, and if you missed a muster, you would get put on report again. I slept through the last muster on the fifth day. I was placed on report, but the division officer tore it up. At my captain's mast he had not said a word against me. That probably helped with the light sentence I received. I couldn't figure out why he liked me so much. I finally figured it out. He was crazier than I was! He was drunk most of the time even out at sea.

The day after the captain's mast, I was transferred to the engine room by the division officer. I was senior to the two MM2s there, so I was third in control after a MM1 and a MMC. My life was better after that. I got along with the whole division. Of course, they all knew about the captain's mast, but they never held it against me. I think they thought I had some kind of "magic" that got me out of trouble, and they hoped I'd bring them good luck.

The first class's name was Mueller. He and I became drinking buddies, and we had a lot of fun playing jokes on the men. The new ones were especially easy prey. We told them that Chief Johnson was losing his hearing from being in the engine room so long, so when they talked to him they had to get up close and yell in his face really loud. Just about every one of them fell for that. The chief knew what we were doing, so he'd play along. I really liked the chief. He was smart, tough, and fair. He did two things I thought were cool. When we were in port, he'd come to quarters every morning and ask if anyone needed any money. He'd pull out a roll of twenty dollar bills, and give people as much money as they wanted. I knew he couldn't have been keeping track of what he'd given out, and I asked him why. He said, "Never give out money if you expect to get it back. It's only money."

Since then, I have tried to maintain that attitude. The other thing he did I really wanted to copy, but the opportunity never came up. In the engine room we had a board to hang coffee cups, and someone had been using his. He called everyone down to the engine room. He took his cup down and said, "This is my coffee cup." Then he unzipped his pants, took out his dick, and rubbed it all around the lip of his cup. Then he said "Any of you assholes feel free to use my cup anytime you want." Then he put his cup back on the board and left. I'm pretty sure nobody ever used his cup again!

The best joke was pulled on an MM2 named Charlie who went drinking with us all the time. We started riding him about the "beer gut" he was getting. He was about six feet two inches and 190 pounds, and actually in pretty good shape. We told him he was getting fat so often that he really became concerned about it. When he was asleep, he would hang his dungaree pants with his belt on the corner of his bunk. About every third night, I would cut about a quarter of an inch off of his belt under the buckle. The next morning I'd start riding him again.

"Damn, Charlie, I thought you were going start getting in shape. You're starting to get a real beer gut on you."

"But I haven't had a beer in over a week, and I'm hardly eating."

"Then maybe you'd better start doing sit-ups. It looks to me like it's getting harder for you to buckle your pants."

He started exercising, and he was hardly eating anything. He looking a little run down, so I had to tell him. I'd cut almost two inches off his belt. Mueller couldn't keep a straight face when he was talking to him. I told him when he was getting dressed one morning.

"Hey Charlie, do me a favor. Take the buckle off of your pants." He did, and then I took the buckle off of my belt. "Look at your belt. Notice anything different between yours and mine?" It was obvious that his had been cut off. It took him a moment to realize what was going on. Mueller was standing there cracking up.

"You assholes! You fucking assholes! I swear to God I'm never going to listen to you assholes ever again."

I bought him a new belt, but he stayed pissed at us for quite a while. We left him alone for a couple of months, and then started pulling things on him again. Charlie just never learned. He fell for them every time. Mueller got transferred the day before we left for the West Pacific. I lost a good buddy, and gained a lot of responsibility. Being the senior MM2, the engine room became mine.

Engine Room Boss

I'll admit that I had reservations about being in charge of an engine room, but it was in pretty good shape for an old ship. It was much better than being under the boiler room. The men knew their jobs, and the chief pretty much left it up to me to run it however I wanted. Under normal steaming conditions, between standing watch and doing the regular work like cleaning and repairs, you could wind up working sixteen-hour days. I had enough of that at the nuclear prototype, so I decided to change the routine. I called the men together and gave them a choice. We could do it my way or the Navy way. My way was this. If they could get the work done during the slack periods on their watches, and as long as everything was up and running and we got "outstanding" on inspections, they could do what they wanted off watch. If, however, something broke down, everyone worked until it was fixed. They chose my way. My way turned out to be pretty good. We got more sleep than anyone else on the ship. I developed my style of leadership. I got the job done my way, but let those above me think it was done their way. I got to test it a couple of weeks later.

We got a new captain the day before we left Long Beach. On his first inspection, he jumped my ass. We had an old rusty pump in the back corner of the engine room. It was tagged "out of service" with a red tag on the inlet and outlet valves, and it had been that way forever. We didn't even know what it was supposed to do.

"Why isn't this pump repaired and ready for use? Everything else in the engine room looks outstanding. This thing looks like it's been neglected for quite a while."

"Yes sir. I've just taken over the engine room, and this pump is definitely on my list of items that need attention. It's not a vital piece of machinery, so I had other things that I felt were more important."

"Everything in this engine room is important, or it wouldn't be here. On my next inspection those tags better be gone. Is that understood?"

"Yes sir. I guarantee that it'll be better than new." When he left I had my men trace the lines under the deck plates. They found that they went nowhere and had even been capped off. Then I had them take the pump apart. It basically had nothing but rust inside it. So I had them put it back together with new bolts and gaskets, and wire brush all the rust from the outside of the pump and the lines above the deck plates. I had them paint it a nice silver color, and take off the red tags. When they were done, it looked great. I really didn't know what I'd do if he told me to start it. Actually I had obeyed his order. The tags were gone.

It was quite a while before he came to the engine room again. He had better things to do. He was busy checking the condition of the ship he had taken over. I hoped he'd forgotten all about that pump. He was going by everything pretty fast. Everything else was running and looked good. We had been getting outstanding on every regular inspection, so he really had no reason to expect problems. My heart skipped a beat when he stopped by the pump.

"Wasn't this the pump that was out of service on my first inspection?"

"Yes sir. We got on it immediately after that. As you said, everything in this engine room is important."

"Good work. If everything continues the way it is now, we'll have a good cruise."

"Thank you, sir. I guarantee that I'll do my best to keep everything as good as it is now." When he continued on his way I realized I had been holding my breath most of the time. I'm surprised I could even talk. Dodged another bullet!

Can you guess what would be our home port in the West Pacific? You got it. It was Subic Bay. I was going home to Olongapo. It was like I had never left. The day before we pulled into port, we had to watch a movie about all the nice sexually transmitted diseases we could get from my Po City girlfriends. The chief gave me money and had me go buy a case of condoms from the ship's store. I'd give a couple of them to everyone going into town. This would be the routine every time we entered any port. Most of the case was gone by the time the cruise was over.

Since I had lived there, I gave the men some advice about how to survive the town. Things like the differences in beer. Every bar had San Miguel beer. However, there were two different bottles that looked almost the same, but were from two different breweries. One was okay, but the other one could have anything in it. They tried to give you the bad one, so you had to know how to tell the difference. I also told them the best bars, most dangerous places, how much to pay for everything, and never to take the best-looking girl because she has every disease. Most important I told them not to get run over by the taxis. It hurts! I never left the base that first time. It was going to be a long cruise, and I was sure I'd have plenty of time to screw up. I was trying, but I knew I could not remain on that ship every time we came into port. I had accepted the fact that I was a fleet sailor. The odds were that I would act like one.

Supertanker

To my surprise, duty on a tanker turned out to be pretty good. We'd be in port for two or three days topping off all of our supplies, and then we'd go back on the line for two or three weeks. We refueled everything from aircraft carriers to gunboats. It wasn't just fuel. We gave them oil, aviation gas, food, mail, ammunition, movies, and just about anything else they might need. Sometimes the gunboat crews were happiest getting a five-gallon tub of ice cream. When we were at refueling or general quarters stations, either the chief or I had to be in the engine room. Refueling a ship was not a simple or safe operation, especially an aircraft carrier in the midst of launching or recovering planes. Bad weather, heavy seas, or dark nights didn't make it any easier. Fighting a war isn't done only in perfect conditions. When you're on a supertanker, it's essentially a very large floating bomb. You really can't afford to make mistakes.

There were times when we were at general quarters for some very long hours, especially when we were refueling the gunboats. They would be lined up for a mile or more beside us, and we stayed on station until they had everything they needed, even if it was just some ice cream. I think I was up for almost seventy-two hours once. I remember going to sleep hanging on a valve wheel. Many times I would sleep in my clothes, because I would either be too tired to take them off, or I knew we would be back at general quarters soon. There were nights when we'd be running very close to the coast. Sometimes when I couldn't sleep, I'd sit up on deck and watch fire fights on shore. With the bomb blasts and tracer fire, it was kind of like watching a Fourth of July celebration until you thought about the guys dying over there.

It was on nights like this that I experienced another example of "military intelligence." We'd be running "blacked out" which meant no lights outside and red lights inside to preserve night vision. Then they'd show a movie up on deck! I decided that the VC must have enjoyed the movies too, or else they'd have blown our asses to hell. I had stopped trying to make sense out of anything the Navy did. Since I was filling a MM1 position, under regular steaming I was in a four hours on and eight hours off watch rotation with Chief Johnson, the BT chief (he and I actually let our past go and worked together), and the division officer filling the other slot. I took a lot of the chief's watches so he could either get some sleep or take care of other business. I could sign his name so well he couldn't tell the difference.

A few times we'd go to Japan instead of Subic Bay. My favorite part of liberty in Japan was going to bath houses. I'd get drunk on my ass, then go get a bath and massage. First they put you in a tub of really hot green water. Then they take you out and sit you on a little wooden stool. After they scrub you all over with a brush, they rinse you off with really cold water. Then came the massage, and it was really great. It never totally sobered me up, but it definitely made me feel good and mellow. I never got into fights in Japan like I did in most other ports.

Just about every time I went to Olongapo I wound up in fights. Even if I took shore patrol duty, I still wound up fighting. The division officer said I healed faster than anyone he'd ever seen. Every time we'd go to sea I'd be beaten to a pulp. By the time we'd go back, I'd be healed and ready to go again. I only had a couple of really bad times. One was a rude awakening even for me. After a night of drinking, I came to. My mind was awake, but I hadn't yet opened my eyes. It felt like someone was sitting on my chest, and I was hugging myself. I couldn't move! Was I buried? Paralyzed? Panic set in, and I wildly opened my eyes and strained to get up. I was yelling and looking all around me. I was on a table, and there was a bright, blinding light right above my eyes. I looked at my chest, and it took a few seconds for my mind to process what I saw. It was a straight jacket. I was in a straight jacket! The panic subsided somewhat, and confusion set in. I realized I was in sick bay on a ship. Was it my ship? What had happened to me? You might think it was impossible not to know why you were in a straight jacket. Honestly, I had no idea what I'd done. A chief corpsman, who was black, came in to the room. I knew him. I was on my ship.

"Do you know me? Do you know where you are?" I nodded my head yes. "Are you going to be calm if I take that off of you?" I again nodded yes, and he took off the jacket.

"What the hell happened to me, chief? What did I do?"

"I don't know for sure. You were totally out of it. The shore patrol brought you to the ship. They said it took several of them to put that jacket on you, and you were still hard to control until you passed out. You came awake once and called me some pretty colorful names. You're lucky I know you didn't mean it. If I had to make a guess, I'd say someone put something in your drink. It's a wonder you're still alive."

I thought that was as good a guess as anything. I know that it had happened to other guys before. Either that or I got careless and drank beer from the bad brewery. Believe it or not, I wasn't put on report. Again, I think the division officer saved my ass, but I never found out for sure.

The other memory I have from this time was of a crazy stunt I pulled. I was very lucky I never got caught. The chief's mess was right above our sleeping compartment. Sometimes when I came back to the ship late, I'd go up and raid the chief's mess for a late night snack. They knew someone was doing it, but I never got caught or told anyone. The last time I tried it, I discovered a lock on the refrigerator. That pissed me off! There were four or five chief's hats on one of the tables, so I took them up on deck and sailed them out into the bay. You can believe there were some pissed off chiefs the next day. If they'd ever found out who had done it, I would be dead. I never told anyone, and I damn sure never went near the chief's mess again.

The cruise was almost over. We were going back on the line one more time before going home. It was January of 1968, and the second day after we left 'Nam the North Koreans captured the spy ship USS Pueblo in international waters. They were towing it to Korea. We turned around and went back to Subic Bay. We quickly topped off our supplies, and took off for Korea with several other ships. We were there until our supplies were depleted, and then we headed back to the U.S. The crew of the Pueblo was still imprisoned in Korea. We were not happy to be leaving them there, but again "military intelligence" was making the decisions. On the way home we did get some good news. The chief had made senior chief (E-8), and I found out I would be receiving orders to compressed gas school. So we both would be leaving the ship. I was told that this was the only cruise that ship had made without breaking down.

Round Eyes Again

Most everyone on the ship was looking forward to being back in the U.S. Me? Not so much. It was going to be hard to adjust to being "normal" again. I was on the ship for another three months or so before I got my orders for compressed gas school. The chief left, and we had a little party for him. We gave him a silver beer mug with his name and rank engraved, so he wouldn't have to worry about anyone using his mug! His replacement was a master chief (E-9). Nobody messes with a master chief. It's as high as you can go in the enlisted ranks. The men were scared he'd be all Navy and by the book, but he turned out to be a pretty good boss. The married guys were always putting in requests for time off to take their wife here or their kids there. I found out the master chief liked horses, so I put in a request for time off to take care of my sick horse. He thought that was funny, so he gave me a couple of days off.

I spent very little time on the ship. Everything was shut down, and I paid Charlie to take most of my duty time. I bought a new 1968 VW Beetle. It was green, and had every accessory available. Of course

I was drunk when I bought it. I liked it though. Even though I knew I shouldn't have a car, it was hard to get anywhere in California without one. I tried not to drive drunk if possible. That was another reason I'd bought a VW. It didn't stand out enough to attract a cop's attention. Mostly I'd get a motel by the bars I usually hung out in, so I could walk from bar to bar.

I still managed to get myself thrown in jail. I was off the ship and I had fifteen days leave and ten days travel time to report to Norfolk, Virginia, for Compressed Gas School. I was staying at the motel for a couple of days before saying good-bye to California. I was drunk as usual one afternoon, and out of the millions of cars in California, I managed to have a collision with a black and white cop car. That alone was bad enough, but the really dumbass part is that I was walking at the time! The cop was stopped at a light, and I had my head in my ass not looking where I was going and walked right into the side of his car. I hit it pretty hard and almost fell on my ass. The cop was young, and I think he was even more surprised than I was that a drunk would walk into the side of his car. He thought it was funny as hell, but he was still going to arrest me. I tried to talk him out of it. I told him I was a sailor, and I would be leaving the state the next day. I even took him to the motel and showed him my orders in the car. He still arrested me. He said it was no big deal. I could get out in the morning and pay my ticket and leave. His last name was Force. On the way to jail I kept trying to get him to tell me his first name. I made several guesses. Was it "Police," "Excessive," or "Magnum"? But he wouldn't tell me. The next morning they let me out and told me where to go to pay the seventy-five dollar ticket. I needed a ride to the motel, and on a wild chance I called my old buddy Mueller's number. I knew he lived somewhere around there, and I thought maybe I could get his wife to come get me. He just happened to be home on leave and answered the phone. He picked me up, took me to pay the ticket, and then back to my car.

He wanted me to come to his house for a while before I left, so I followed him there. Late that afternoon when I was getting ready to leave, he asked me to take him down to the store a couple of blocks from his house. I took him to the store, and on the way back we were stopped at a light. He told me to make a U-turn. I pointed out the big sign that said "No U-turns." He said he'd lived there his whole life, and nobody paid any attention to those signs. So I made a U-turn. Three cars behind me was a cop car. As soon as I made the turn, I looked to the left and directly into Force's eyes.

I said, "Shit," and just pulled over and stopped. Sure enough, here came the red lights behind me. I got out of the car, and was standing there with my hands out for the handcuffs as Force walked up.

"Webster, is that you? What in the hell are you doing here? You're supposed to be on your way to Virginia."

"Force, I swear I was on my way. That idiot in the car made me do it!" Force walked back to my car and gave Mueller a long look, then came back to me.

"I can't believe that two days in a row you do something that I just can't ignore. At least you're sober today. I'm not going to bust you two days in a row, but I don't want to ever see you again. Now get your ass out of my patrol area."

"Believe me, as soon as I take that idiot home I'm out of here." We laughed and shook hands, and I got back into the car. Mueller asked what all the laughing was about. I told him "I gave him your name and address, and he's going to send the ticket to you." I took him home and immediately left the state. This was the second time I had been run out of town before sundown! Mueller's probably still waiting on the ticket.

East Coast Again

Driving a VW wasn't quite the same as a GTO, but I didn't waste any time driving cross-country again. I drove nonstop until I got to my hometown. I don't remember how long it took me, but I remember having a hard time staying awake going through Texas. Again, it was just sheer luck that I never got a ticket or had a wreck. At least I was sober. If I had been drinking, I would never have made it in one piece.

Paoli was no different than I had left it. My parents had repaired their house from my last visit. I'm surprised they'd even let me stay there again. Parents are funny that way. I was determined to make this visit better than the last. I did better, but of course I just couldn't stay out of trouble completely.

My buddy James thought it was pretty funny that he had my GTO, and I was driving a pregnant roller skate—his nickname for the VW. He let me drive the GTO, and that led to another time in lockup. A guy a few years older than us had just bought a new Mustang 289. He was in a bar bragging about what a hot car it was. Of course the subject of a drag race came up. I told him he was outclassed by the GTO, but of course he wasn't going to take my word for it. He wanted to race, and he wanted to bet on it. James said he could use some easy money, so they agreed to two hundred dollars and a couple of cases of beer. It was no contest. We blew his doors off.

He paid off the bet except for the beer, since the liquor stores were closed. The next day was Sunday, and you couldn't buy beer in Indiana on Sunday. He said we could go to Kentucky and get the beer. I wasn't going to drive to Kentucky. He said he'd drive, and I could just ride along. I really didn't want to go, but I was a dumbass and didn't have anything else to do. After we got the beer, he wanted to stop at a bar. I didn't think it was a good idea, but I wasn't driving.

"We're a long way from home. Do you think you should be driving and drinking down here? There are a lot more cops around here. This isn't Paoli."

"We'll just have a couple. I've done this several times. I'll be fine." So we stopped at a bar he knew. We had two or three beers and shot a couple of games of pool. We were in pretty good shape when we left there. We hadn't driven long when he wanted to stop again.

"I know a couple of the barmaids at this other place. They usually give me several drinks free. We won't stay long."

He was right. They knew him there, and we got several free drinks. We didn't, however, have a couple and leave. We were there quite a while, and it was dark when we left for home in his Mustang. His driving was pretty wild. I tried to get him to slow down and be more careful, but he wouldn't listen. We never made it past New Albany, Indiana. The cops got us, and he went to jail for a DUI. Since I was too drunk to drive (and a little mouthy), they took me in with him. I was in uniform, so they didn't charge me with anything when they let me out the next morning. I had to hitchhike back to Paoli. I called his family and told them where he was so they could bail him out. I didn't ever see him again or find out what happened. I never told my parents about that little adventure. A couple of days later I left for Norfolk. Again I left my car home and flew back. I wasn't going to be in Norfolk for that long, and I didn't know where I'd be going from there. At least I didn't get run out of town this time. I was finally getting the education that I had been promised when I extended my enlistment. It had been a hard fight, but I got three of the four things (two promotions and the school) I was promised. Only the sub pay and pro pay remained. I still had three years to work on getting them.

I mostly stayed straight during my time at Compressed Gas School. The school was hard enough that I had to study, and it was wintertime. Since I didn't have wheels, it wasn't that much fun to walk to the bars in the cold and snow. It was similar to nuclear power school, but nowhere near as stressful. The tests involved drawing all the systems, but they were not as involved as drawing every system on a submarine. I actually liked the school. Working in a gas plant was going to be much better than an engine room. Upon graduation, I received orders to the USS Enterprise CVAN-65. At least I couldn't bitch about not getting a combat ship. I was going to the largest warship in the world.

The "Big E"

I had ten day's travel time and took five day's leave, so I had plenty of time before reporting aboard. I was going to fly from Virginia to California, and then to Hawaii to pick up the ship in Pearl Harbor. I remember going to the airport. I had several hours before my flight, so I spent the time waiting in the airport bar. I met another sailor there. He was going to be on my flight, but he was getting off in Louisville, Kentucky. It was the first of two stops the flight was making on the way to San Francisco.

We were pretty drunk when we boarded, and we were given seats in the last row of the plane. While we were waiting to take off he pulled a bottle of scotch out of his travel bag. He asked me if I had ever drunk scotch and milk. Not only had I not done it, I had never even thought of it. He assured me I would like it, so we had the stewardess bring us a couple of glasses of milk. He was right. It was pretty good, but by then I was drunk enough to drink anything.

By the time we reached Louisville, we had finished most of the bottle. I could tell the stewardess was wondering why we had a sudden thirst for milk. Then he had another good idea. Since I had fifteen days, why didn't I spend a couple of days with him? His girlfriend had a lot of nice friends who liked sailors. So I got off the plane in Louisville.

That was the last thing I remember until I woke up on a couch in a trailer. I had no idea where I was. There was a guy sleeping on the floor, and two other guys in the back bedrooms. I had never seen any of them in my life. It was around 9 AM and it looked sunny out, so I opened the door and looked outside. We were out on a country road, and although I couldn't believe it, I thought I knew where it was. It looked like the country about one mile from our farm in Paoli. While I was trying to make some sense out of it, the guy sleeping on the floor woke up and came outside. I know I must have looked like an idiot standing there staring at him. He didn't say anything, so I had to ask.

"I know you're going to think this is a weird question, but who are you guys, and where the hell am I?"

"What do you mean? You really don't know where you are?" He started laughing. "You're in Paoli. Where the hell did you think you were?" The other two guys heard us talking and came outside. "He doesn't know where he is. Can you believe that shit?" The other guys were looking at me like I was from another planet. One of them was just shaking his head, like he thought he was dreaming.

"We picked you up hitchhiking from Louisville two days ago. You told us you'd been staying with another sailor in Louisville. You told us you were from Paoli. You never said why you were coming here, and you've been staying here and drinking with us ever since. You don't remember any of this? Man, that's some freaky weird shit."

They told me their names, but I didn't know any of them. They were a lot younger than me. They thought I was funny as hell, but I wasn't so amused. I had one of them take me to my parents' house. They, too, were surprised to see me. My dad asked me why I was there, and I told him I didn't know I *was* there! He didn't believe me. He said, "Nobody can get that drunk." I told him he could believe what he wanted, but the only thing I knew was that I had left Virginia, and I was supposed to be in California, and Paoli was the last place I wanted to be. I never convinced him. I took a bus back to Louisville, and continued my trip to the ship. The sad part was that it never even bothered me that much. Things like this were becoming normal for me.

I arrived in Hawaii sometime around midnight. I remember that there were several fountain-type drink dispensers all over the airport. They were filled with pineapple juice, and you could drink all you wanted for free. I drank so much it almost made me sick! By the time I got to the ship at Pearl Harbor it was the middle of the night. It seemed that ever since boot camp, I arrived to each duty station in the middle of the night. Standing on the dock looking at the ship, I was overwhelmed by the sheer size of it. I had seen aircraft carriers before, but this ship seemed larger than life. It was amazing! After just looking for several minutes, I made myself go up the gangplank and I reported aboard. I knew my time on this ship was going to be an adventure. They took me down a few decks to a small berthing compartment and found me a bunk, but I was so wound up I didn't get any sleep that night.

The next morning one of the men took me to the main chow hall for breakfast. It, too, seemed huge, and the food was good. It was much better than on the tanker, and you could eat all you wanted. After breakfast, a guide took me to the A Division office. The division officer was a full lieutenant. He took my records, and had someone take me to the aft compressed gas plant. That was when I met Chief Roberts.

"Wel-wel-welcome a-a-board. It-it's about time we go-g-got a ne-new operator." The chief had a really bad stuttering problem.

I thought, *this is going to be interesting.* Between my speech defect and the chief's stuttering, we should have interesting conversations. He took me to the forward plant and introduced me to the other men. Both plants were basically the same, but the aft one was smaller. I was going to work in the aft plant. I would be the third operator with the chief and a MM1. We continued to tour all of A Division's work areas. It was a slow process waiting for the chief to do the introductions, but as the morning progressed I realized I was not noticing his stutter as much. By the time we finished it was almost noon. The chief said we would go to the EM club for lunch, and I could see the rest of the base.

On the way back to the ship I had my second "twilight zone" experience. As we were walking back to the ship, I heard explosions and machine gun fire. I looked up and saw two World War II Japanese Zero fighter planes. They were about fifty feet off the ground, and I could see the pilots. They had Japanese rising sun scarves on their heads! I looked up over the mountains, and there were several formations turning to make for the ships in the docks. I looked back at the ships, and there were fires, explosions, and water spouts from bombs missing. All of this time, we were just walking along. My head was turning wildly, and I'm sure my eyes were popping out of my head.

I looked at the chief, and he didn't even seem to notice anything. I stopped and said, "Damn, chief, what the hell is going on? Don't you see this? Am I just crazy, or are we in the twilight zone?" I thought he was going to piss his pants he was laughing so hard. Obviously he had seen it too, except he knew they were making the movie *Tora! Tora! Tora!* That was the weirdest feeling I've ever experienced. Then I understood how those guys felt on the morning of the Pearl Harbor attack, and I'll never forget it. Of course when we got back to the ship everyone soon heard the chief's story of my reaction. My first day was starting off great. Now everyone knew I was an idiot.

As if that wasn't bad enough, my day went downhill from there. As soon as we got back to the ship, I was called to report to the A Division office. From the aft plant it took me about half an hour to find the office. Then they gave me the good news. When they sent my records to personnel, someone noticed that I was nuclear qualified and had told the M division officer. They wanted to assign me to the M Division in the engine room.

Why wasn't I surprised? It makes perfect military sense. They spent one hundred thousand dollars to train me for something, and then they told me to forget it. Believe me, that was one order I followed to the letter. Two years later, they spent money to train me for something else. Then they told me I'm not going to do that job. At that moment I would rather have been in the twilight zone. It would have made better sense. I wanted to scream.

Even though I would get pro pay if I worked in the engine room, I wanted to work in the gas plants. I'd done my time in engine rooms. So I made my case to the lieutenant. They needed me in the gas plants. There were not that many qualified operators in the Navy. There were, however, many nuclear machinist mates and they could find someone else.

I said, "You're two operators short. You're not going to let the M division officer just take me, are you? Does he have more power than you?" I think that did it. He went to talk to the engineering officer and I got to stay in A Division. I really don't know what I'd have done if it had gone the other way. I'd probably have set a new record for getting thrown off a ship!

There was a reason the ship was in Hawaii. The flight deck of a carrier is one of the most dangerous work environments in the world, especially during combat flight operations. One mistake can have severe consequences. Before deployment to Vietnam, they have practice missions to make sure everything and everyone functions properly. They fly a simulated combat mission and bomb a small Hawaiian island. On the morning of the last practice run, it turned into much more than a practice mission.

The ship was at general quarters at 0800. The planes were loaded with five hundred pound bombs and missiles. Somehow one of the men operating a jet engine starter set off a five hundred pound bomb. That started an unimaginable firestorm that could have destroyed the ship. The exploding five hundred pound bombs were sometimes going off in multiples. They blew holes down through the decks. Flaming jet fuel then streamed down into the interior of the ship, setting fire to everything in its path. A missile cooked off and went into the ship's island, which houses the flight observation and control areas. It lodged in a firemain, but it didn't have time to arm itself, so it didn't explode. The flight deck was a total hell of explosions and fire. Everything was recorded on the flight deck cameras. Men ran up to one of the fires with a hose and then a bomb exploded. The front men on the hose disappeared in a blast of fire, smoke, and flying metal from the bomb. The other men retreated for a few seconds until the blast subsided, then picked up the hose and charged the fire again, only to be cut down by another bomb blast. Firemains were cut by the blasts. Sometimes men were charging a fire with an empty hose. One of the flight team members hooked up a burning F-4 Phantom and drove it over the side. Because of heroic measures from flight deck and damage control personnel, the ship was saved, but we lost twenty-seven men and fifteen aircraft.

The aft gas plant is on the starboard side of the ship on the hanger bay level. It's only four levels down from the flight deck. Like most areas below the flight deck, there is no way to see what's going on outside the space. There aren't portholes to see outside. It is not a cruise ship. If your general quarters station is in a lower level space, the only way you know what's going on is from the ship's communication headphones. The aft plant was like being in a submarine when it was depth charged. It was a hot, cramped, dark space. On this day, the air conditioning was off, and the lighting came from emergency battle lanterns. The concussions from the five hundred pound bombs going off sent anything that wasn't secured flying through the plant. The plant was shut down, but there were 750 gallons of liquid oxygen in the storage tank. It could not be dumped. The side of the ship where the emergency dump valve was located was ablaze from burning jet fuel. It was sheer luck that none of the blasts got to the plant.

With all of the bomb blasts going off, one of the men, whose name was Karl, was trying to look cool and not scared. He started to get a cup of coffee just as another bomb went off. The coffee pot jumped off the bench from the concussion, and his face turned as white as a sheet. He and I later became drinking buddies, and I still remember him retelling the story of what happened next. The headphones were manned by the chief. Every time Karl and I were out drinking he would say, "Webster, I admit that I was scared, but I was doing okay until I heard the chief on the phones. He never stuttered once. I knew then that we were going to die." He was right. In all my time on that ship, I never again heard the Chief complete a sentence without stuttering.

Because of the extensive damage done by the fire, we were in the yards at Pearl Harbor for quite a while. The yard workers said they hadn't seen anything like that since World War II. I don't remember how long the repairs took, but as soon as they were finished we completed the sea trials and headed for the West Pacific.

Crossing the Pacific on this ship was different than the others. It is totally amazing that something that big can move as fast as it can. With the air wing on board, we had around fifty-five hundred men, almost twice the population of my hometown. It was a floating city, and we had everything we needed. We had laundry service, a ship's store, and a gym. There was always a movie showing somewhere, and we even had our own TV station. There were four chow halls, plus the first class mess, the chief's mess, and the officer's mess. The food was good. We had steak and lobster twice a week. I had never eaten lobster until then. Sometimes the line for the main chow hall would go up a couple of decks and all around the hanger bay. It could take an hour or more waiting in line. That gave me an incentive to make first class. They went to the head of the line, and they had their own mess.

Each bunk had its own locker, light, and air conditioning. The small berthing compartment I was in only had about twenty guys. It was for the guys who maintained the catapults, and since they worked weird shifts, the lights were out all the time. I was told to move into the A Division compartment, which was a lot bigger with about 150 guys, but I was happy where I was, so I just ignored the order. That almost got me into big trouble later on.

I hadn't been on the ship very long before my time as an MM2 was up, and I was eligible to take the first class test. During my whole enlistment, all I heard was bitching about me making rank without having to take a test. The other guys said I didn't know anything since all of my promotions were the result of college or reenlistment. Then I made first class the first time I took the test, and that put a stop to the bitching.

Being an MM1 made my life much better. No more standing in chow lines. Another benefit was being able to wear civilian clothes on and off the ship. When I got into the first class mess I found some of my old buddies. Two were from the Markab. The other one was from my company in boot camp, and he was now a nuke working in the engine room. It was kind of funny seeing these guys after so long. The guys from the Markab couldn't believe I was still in the Navy and a first class. Making first class also saved me from my division officer. He had ordered me to move into the A Division berthing compartment. I still didn't do it, and he was going to have my ass. Then, right after I made first class, they decided to move all of the A Division's First Class into the compartment I was in. It saved my ass. He was seriously going to have me for failing to obey a direct order.

Carrier pilots, both Navy and Marines, are the best pilots in the world. Landing on a moving carrier under perfect conditions is very difficult. When you add bad weather, heavy seas, black nights, and being shot all to hell it becomes almost impossible, but they do it. Some of the planes would have holes so big you could put your hand through them. We had F-4 Phantoms, A-6 Intruders, A-7 Corsairs, and a couple of big Vigilante spy photo planes. On our first mission we lost one of the Vigilantes. It got over into Cambodia, and it was targeted by a surface to air missile. Unfortunately, both men were lost. I can still see their footlockers sitting on the flight deck to be flown home.

Most of the time on the line we were flying missions twenty-four hours a day. It never took that long for them to make a strike. From where we were it only took about twenty minutes for the aircraft to reach their targets. Most of our pilots had already flown missions in 'Nam. They followed the rules of engagement, but they used all the tricks they had learned the hard way to kill the enemy and survive. Sometimes if they weren't flying missions, we'd pull a target behind the ship for gunnery practice. Damn they were good! I was glad I wasn't the one they were attacking. Like I said before, they brought back some planes that were shot up so badly it was hard to believe they would still fly. We only lost one other plane on that cruise. It was an A-7 fighter and the pilot almost made it back before he had to eject. He was picked up and was okay.

In April of 1969, I got to go to Korea again. This time the North Koreans had shot down a reconnaissance plane over international waters and immediately we had orders to sail. We had to wait for our planes that were out on a strike to be recovered before we took off for North Korea. We had briefings on North Korean weapon systems, and we took on ammunition all the way there. We had bombs stacked everywhere. I ate in the first class mess leaning on a two thousand pound bomb. There were three other carrier battle groups with us. Looking at the vast formations from on the observation level, I was reminded of a World War II movie. Even though we were fighting a war in Vietnam, I had the feeling this was going to be different. The pilots were looking forward to being able to fight without all the restraints placed on them. But as usual, the *Enterprise* did a lot of saber rattling, but never did anything.

We stayed stationed there for about a month after the others went back to 'Nam. During that time I didn't even go topside very often. It was too cold and there was nothing to see. Eventually we also went back to the line and continued strikes on Viet Nam. When we returned to Subic Bay we off-loaded some of the extra ordnance. A first class gunners mate told me we were authorized to carry six nuclear weapons, but we off-loaded many more than that. If the other carriers had similar loads, it's a good thing the Koreans never escalated the situation. If they had, we would not be having any more trouble with North Korea!

At some point following that mission, we went into port in Singapore. That was a pretty wild liberty port! We were only there for three days, but it was long enough for me to find some more trouble. On our last day another guy and I went to a bar in a rough section of Singapore. We were sitting with a couple of bar girls when a guy came up. He whispered something to the girl who was with my buddy. She got this scared look on her face. My buddy asked her what was wrong.

"He said I should tell you that you shouldn't stay with him," she pointed to me, "Or you will die too!" We both became very alert at that.

"Webster, what the hell have you done now? I swear to God if you get me killed I'll kill you myself. Shit! You know what I mean. We've only been here three days. Who have you pissed off enough to kill you?"

"Hell I don't know. Last night when we were waiting on the liberty boat a couple of sailors got into a fight with some taxi drivers. I got in the middle of that. I only hit one guy. Then they took off. I guess losing a fight really pisses them off."

"You're really a crazy dumbass. These people will kill you for a dollar. If you hurt one of them, you're in deep shit. What the hell are you going to do? There's over a million guys out there and they all look alike. If you don't come up with a plan, you're a dead man."

"This is really great. Now I'm going to cause an international incident!" Several of the bar girls had heard about it, and they were all grouped around us talking a mile a minute. They wanted to go outside and find the guy. I didn't want them to escalate the situation. If the guys out there knew I'd been warned, they might come into the bar after me. I was thinking fast. Then I had an idea.

"Does the bar have a telephone? I need to make a call." One of the girls took me to the phone and helped me make the call. I don't think I could have done it without her help. The phone operator didn't understand English. Singapore was under British control, and I remembered seeing armed British military police a couple of times. I called their office and told them what was happening. They told me to stay in the bar, and they would come to get me. I went back to the table. I kept an eye on every man in the bar, and made sure I never turned my back to any of them. There were several girls at the table with my buddy. I could tell he was really nervous too.

"Who the hell did you call? Did you call the ship?"

"Hell no, I don't want the ship involved in this. I called the British MPs. They're coming to get me. Just keep an eye on the guys in the bar until they get here."

"How the hell did you think to call them? I can't believe the shit you do. I thought some of the stories about you were bullshit. If you get out of this alive, I'll be a believer."

It seemed longer, but after about thirty minutes, two big British Marines with machine guns came into the bar. You can believe I was very happy to see them! I got up and went to meet them. It was unusual to be happy to see the police coming for me.

"What's the problem, mate? Got yourself in bit of a situation, have you?"

"It seems that way. I'd sure appreciate it if you could help me with it."

"It's no trouble at all, mate. We're always happy to help out our American chums." They took me out and we got into a jeep with one of them on each side of me. There was quite a crowd outside. I saw one guy who had a bandage on his nose and was pretty beat up. I figured he was probably involved. I waved good-bye to him as we drove off. He looked really pissed.

They took me back to their station. One of them asked me what I was doing out in that part of town. It seems if I had been killed there, I wouldn't have been the first. They told me I didn't have to go back to the ship if I didn't want to. I told them I thought I'd had enough fun, and if they'd give me a lift to the dock, I would be happy to return to the ship. Once again I'd escaped a dangerous situation. I wondered when my luck was going to run out.

We returned to the line and continued our normal strikes on Vietnam. Before long it was time to return to the U.S. On my last liberty in Olongapo I said good-bye to old friends again. I didn't think I'd ever see them again, but I had learned not to take anything for granted. My girlfriend who owned the restaurant wanted to come to the U.S. We talked about it, but I never really thought it would happen. It turned out I was right about that.

Of course I couldn't leave Olongapo without getting into trouble one last time. I was drunk and lost track of time, and I was still in the restaurant past curfew. I had no choice but to turn myself in to the shore patrol. I had to get back to the ship since we were leaving the next day. So they put me on report and took me back to the ship.

The next day I was supposed to go see the engineering officer. The chief thought it was pretty funny. He said, "Tha-tha-that man's a full co-com-commander and you can't te-tell him a st-st-story he hasn't heard."

"We'll see about that," I said. I bet him fifty dollars that I wouldn't be sent to captain's mast. Then I went to tell the commander "a story he hadn't heard." When I got to his office he looked like he wasn't in a good mood. I began to have doubts that I could pull this off. The only good part was that I hadn't been in trouble on this ship. He only had the one report to read.

"Can't you tell time sailor? You're a first class petty officer. I shouldn't have to waste my time on things like this. You should be setting an example. Do you want to keep your stripes? What do you have to say for yourself?"

"It's not an excuse, sir. But I do have a reason I was late." He continued to stare at me.

"I was in a restaurant in town saying good-by to the owners. Their son, Tony, (I had to give him a name) was my roommate when he was an exchange student at Purdue. Since I knew I would probably never see him again, I lost track of time talking over old times. I was only fifteen minutes late, and yes, sir, I would like to keep my stripes. I can promise you that you'll never have to see me again, sir." His expression hadn't changed all the time I was talking. I began to think the chief was right. It was possible I had met someone I couldn't bullshit.

"You're right. That's not an excuse. It is somewhat understandable. Just be clear on one thing. If I ever see you here again, you will go to captain's mast and lose some stripes. Am I making myself clear?"

"Yes sir. Thank you, sir. You will never have to waste your time on me again."

"For your sake I hope you're right. Get out of my sight and go back to work." I went back to work, and collected fifty bucks from the chief. He never bet me on anything again.

When we sailed under the Golden Gate Bridge, I still had about two years left on my enlistment. We were going to be in San Francisco for a short time, and then we were going to the Naval Shipyard Portsmouth, Virginia, to have a major overhaul. They had one of the only two dry docks that were big enough to hold the ship. If you think the ship looks big on water, you should see it out of the water. It was absolutely unbelievable! We were going to be there a year or more. They were going to refuel the reactors, and they would be good for twenty five more years. Most of the work on the gas plants had to be done by civilians, so I wondered what I'd be doing.

The ship was too big to go through the Panama Canal, so we would be sailing around Cape Horn at the tip of South America. The highlight of this trip would be the "shellback" initiation crossing the Equator. Originally intended as a test of endurance by the Vikings, this initiation was for sailors to prove themselves worthy of entering the realm of King Neptune, ruler of the sea. Those who have not been initiated are called "polliwogs." This is another thing you have to experience to appreciate. Please believe me that the Vikings were very lucky they weren't on an aircraft carrier with thirty-five hundred men aboard.

It starts at breakfast. The shellbacks eat steak and eggs. Polliwogs get some shit I can't even describe. We had to wear t-shirts with a "P" on the front and back, and our pants inside out and backward. They took us in groups—on our knees bowing with our heads on the deck—up to the flight deck on a flight elevator. We then had to crawl on our hands and knees through a seemingly never-ending shillelagh line. They beat the hell out of us with belts, wrapped towels, pieces of fire hose. I couldn't decide what hurt the most. The many hits I received definitely hurt, but crawling on the steel deck was killing my knees. We had to kiss the royal baby's belly, which was a really fat guy with grease on his belly. Then we were dunked in a coffin filled with lard, grease, and fog foam. Then came the royal doctor with some foul tasting medicine, followed by the royal dentist with more foul shit. The royal barber gave us a really great haircut, and then we had to crawl through a garbage chute that I thought I was going to die in. It was a tunnel made out of tarps that they had filled with garbage and had water from a fire hose running through it. It would have been hard enough just to crawl on your stomach through the collapsed tarp, but the heat, water, and garbage made it was almost impossible for me. I didn't know if I was going to suffocate, drown, or have a heat stroke. Finally at the end we were plunged into a water-filled tank to symbolize the final purification of a slimy polliwog. It is something I will never forget. I am a shellback!

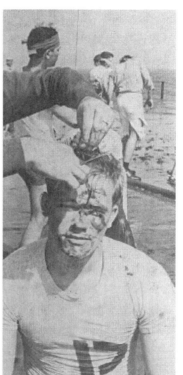

All of this to get a little card.

Around Cape Horn we went through some of the most treacherous waters in the world, the Strait of Magellan. In the past, many sailing ships failed and were sunk there. We had good weather and had no problems, and we were heading for Rio de Janeiro. We were going to have four days liberty there, and I was determined not to be a drunken sailor. Amazingly, I never took a drink the whole time. So even though I had to go alone, I rented a taxi and went to all the famous places. It is definitely a beautiful place with white sand beaches and women everywhere. I had to listen to the stories from the other guys on the ship, and they were having some wild times. They kept trying to get me to go along, but I never gave in for once. If we had been there more than four days, I most likely would have joined them.

I wasn't looking forward to being in Norfolk again, and it turned out to be some really bad times. I went back to being a drunken sailor again. It was either that or stay on the ship all the time. The only places the other sailors went were bars. I just accepted that as long as I was a sailor, I was going to be drinking. I just didn't have a strong enough will to avoid it. Soon after we arrived, I took some leave and went home to get my car. Nothing there was interesting, so I managed not to get run out of town. On the way back to Norfolk, I finally got a speeding ticket. I think the cop was surprised a VW would go eighty-five miles per hour. I was lucky I wasn't in the GTO.

Being in the shipyard was as boring as I thought it was going to be. Since civilians were doing most of the work on the plants, we basically had nothing to do. I rented a house in Virginia Beach with one of the guys from the catapult gang. One of the roughest bars in town was about half a mile from our house. It became our second home. Several bars in Newport News were favorite hangouts also. Then there was an after-hours place called the Fleet Reserve Club. We went there when the bars closed at midnight, and drank there until 3 AM. It was a rough place, and I again added to my reputation for fighting.

I worked as bouncer there sometimes, and that's how I lost my front teeth. To get in you had to ring a bell for the door to be opened. One night I threw a guy out. When I opened the door a little later, he met me with a lead pipe right in the mouth. It knocked me back into the pool table inside the door, and when he came in I swung a pool cue at him. We both went to the same hospital that night. My four upper front teeth were basically gone. I don't know what happened to him. It only took a few seconds to lose the teeth, and three months or so to get them replaced.

I bought a new car, which proved to be another mistake. It was a red Opal GT. It looked kind of like a little Corvette. It drew a lot more attention than a VW Beetle. This is not a good thing when you're a drunken sailor. It didn't take long until I got busted for a DUI one night leaving the Fleet Reserve Club. I lost my driver's license for one year, was fined three hundred dollars, and got thirty days in jail, which was suspended. I deserved it. They could have got me for drunk driving any day for several years. It was just dumb luck that I never killed myself or someone else. I wasn't alone. While we were in Norfolk, around two hundred men from the ship lost their licenses. My roommate got busted when he went home on leave in Ohio. He had to take thirty days leave and do his jail time there. I didn't drive a car again for over three years.

To my credit, I didn't drive, and I really tried to stop drinking. I sold the car to a chief from one of the deck divisions on the ship. I told him he could pay me a certain amount each month until it was paid off. He asked me if I wanted him to sign something, and I said it wasn't necessary. He said, "What if I don't pay you?"

"If you don't pay me, I'll kill you. Ask around," I said. He never missed a payment.

I made a real effort to stop drinking, but since everyone I knew went to the bars every day, I had to do everything alone. Going to movies and bowling by your self gets old fast. I think I lasted about six weeks. My roommate told me he was glad I finally started drinking again because he couldn't stand me sober. I was the same way. I couldn't stand drunks if I was sober, and I couldn't stand sober people when I was drunk.

Not long after I became a drunk again, my roommate and I had a really funny adventure. His father bought into a cosmetics company, and since we dated women from the Fort Monroe Army base, he wanted us to get them to sell to the Women's Army Corps on the base. Like always, there was a catch. Before the company would let us be distributors, we had to go to a class to learn how to put on the makeup. So one Saturday morning there we were. The two of us and about twenty women at a class on how to put on makeup. Of course we were drunk, and it had to be one of the funniest times in my life. The cotton balls kept getting caught in my beard. I had makeup and shreds of cotton all over my face. Everyone was laughing so hard the class was a total bust. I really wish I had gotten some pictures of us. I don't think we wound up selling much, but it was worth it just for the memory of that day.

We were in the yards longer than expected. They had problems refueling the reactors. I was definitely ready to leave. Most of my time there had been bad news. Unfortunately, I still had time to get into more trouble. The American Legion in Norfolk was one of my regular hangouts. Like the Fleet Reserve Club, to enter you had to ring a bell, and then a doorman let you in. The doorman there was a good guy, and I got to know him pretty well. That was usually one place I had never had any problems with anyone, but that all changed one Saturday night.

Another guy and I were there having a pretty good time. I was drunk, but he got really plowed. He was so out of it I decided to take him back to the ship around midnight. I had the doorman call us a taxi, and we went outside to wait for it. He was so bad he could hardly stand up, so I had him sit on the hood of the car while we were waiting. We were in civilian clothes, and while we were waiting, two sailors in uniform came from around the side of the building. They never said anything to me, but for some reason they started messing with him. They were mouthing off and pushing him, so I told them to leave him alone and be on their way. That got them focused on me, and then they starting calling me several not so nice names. They were young and drunk, and I really didn't want any trouble with them.

I told them, "Be smart guys and walk away." They didn't listen, and they both started toward me. I hit the one in front, he fell into the other one, and they both went down. They got up and took off running around the side of the building.

I thought that was the end of it, but two minutes later about twenty-five sailors in uniform came running around the corner. There were two or three shore patrol with them. They came running at us screaming, and I found myself in the wildest fight I'd ever been in. They attacked us, and then they started fighting each other and the shore patrol too. I yanked my buddy off the car and fought my way to the door. I had him in one hand, and I was ringing the bell and fighting with my other hand and my feet.

When the door opened I threw him inside, jumped in behind him, and slammed the door. I told the doorman not to open the door for anyone. While I was telling him what was going on outside, my buddy woke up and kept trying to go outside. He wouldn't stop, so I had to hit him. That stopped him. I picked him up and the doorman took us to an office in the back. He told us to stay there until he came back.

All hell was breaking loose outside. It took police from Norfolk and Newport News, the Virginia State Police, and the shore patrol to break it up. All of the sailors were from a deck division on the Enterprise. They were having a division party in a private room at the Legion. There was a whole school bus full of them, and they were all drunk. A Norfolk police officer chased one of them onto the bus, and three sailors went in after him. The four sailors almost beat the cop to death. All four of them got nine years in prison for that. It was around 3 AM by the time it was all over.

The doorman came and got us and took us back to the ship. The next day my buddy's face was all swollen and purple from where I'd hit him. He said he'd never been hit so hard. I felt really bad about it, but if he'd gone back outside, he could have been killed.

It was tense on the ship. Nobody knew for sure who we were; we were in civilian clothes, and we kept a low profile for a long time. I was called to talk to the division officer. He asked me if I was involved in it, and I was smart enough to say I knew nothing about it. Nothing more was ever said about it. I continued to watch my back for a long time. We finally completed the overhaul and headed back to San Francisco. I never wanted to see Virginia again.

We were going back the way we'd come, but the trip back would be a little different. I was a shellback, so I didn't have to go through another painful initiation. I'd had my fill of hitting or being hit, so I volunteered to stand watch. I never took part in the beating of the polliwogs.

When we arrived in Rio, I hit the bars and nightclubs this time. The stories had been right. It was definitely a wild city. I made up for the last time. The beaches and the women were great. Most of the women didn't speak English, but that never seemed to be a problem.

It did lead to a funny situation. I was walking down the beach with the guy I had been in boot camp with, when we came to this beautiful girl laying topless in the sun. He stopped and stood there staring at her. I thought, *this ought to be interesting*. It was.

"Hi. My name's Danny. I'm an American sailor. I think you're really beautiful, and your boobs are the prettiest I've ever seen." She just looked at him and smiled. He looked at me and smiled. I never said a word. Then he looked back at her.

"Not only do I think your boobs are pretty, I think your whole body looks great. I'd like to rub lotion all over you. Actually, I'd like to lick all the sweat off of you." She kind of arched her eyebrows and continued smiling at him. He looked at me grinning broadly.

"Isn't this great? She doesn't have the slightest idea what I'm saying to her." He turned back to her and went into some graphic detail of a few sexual acts he'd like to perform on her. When he stopped talking, she stood up and walked really close to him.

"I'm from Cleveland." I wish you could have seen the look on his face. I really had never seen a sailor blush before. She was a schoolteacher from Cleveland on vacation. She must have liked what he said, because he spent the next two days with her.

The last day we were there was the first day of their Mardi Gras. The celebration there makes the one in New Orleans look like a Sunday school picnic. Rio was the only place I've ever been that I'd like to visit again.

Going around Cape Horn was different this time, too. We hit bad weather and some very rough seas. We took water over the flight deck! When we got to San Francisco there were big dents in the bow of the ship. I knew then why so many sailing ships never made it through the strait.

Shortly after we arrived in San Francisco, the Navy started a new policy. They wanted to reduce the size of the Navy, so they were giving three month "early out" discharges. I couldn't believe it. I never thought I'd get out, and now I would be discharged three months early! I know it's hard to believe, but I actually considered staying in. I told them I'd "ship over" for sub school, the PBRs, or shore duty anywhere outside the U.S., preferably in Vietnam. Of course they wouldn't guarantee any of these. As I had learned, the guarantees didn't mean a thing anyway, so I took the discharge.

The day I got out I went to a bar with the two guys I was with on the Markab. I had about thirteen hundred dollars, and the party was on me.

"You'll be back before we leave on the next cruise. What else are you going to do? In spite of all the bitching, you're a lifer. You like being a sailor."

"I've known you guys a long time. You know all of the shit I've pulled. You know I won't live long if I continue doing this. Look at us. It's two o'clock in the afternoon, and we're already drunk on our asses."

"You'll be back. You won't fit in with civilians anymore."

"You're probably right, but I'm going to give it a try. I'm not going to work at the Paoli Handle Factory. If I can't find something better, I'll be back. You guys are going to miss me. You've got to admit I've given you several good sea stories to tell."

"That a fact. You're one crazy dumbass. See you in a couple of months."

They left me at the bar and went back to the ship. Three days later I was drunk and broke, and some hooker in Oakland had made off with most everything I had. I called the first class mess on the ship, and one of my buddies came and got me. He loaned me the money for a plane ticket to Indiana, and drove me to the airport. I had no luggage, had been wearing the same clothes for three days, hadn't shaved, and paid for the ticket in cash. In today's world I would never be let on a plane. Even then they gave me some questioning looks.

So after seven years I was back at home in Paoli. I was twenty-seven years old. I was an alcoholic, had no money or anything else, and didn't have a clue what I was going to do. I didn't need any sunglasses. It was 1971 and my future wasn't looking too bright.

A Summer of Change

After a week or so, I had completely sobered up and started to think about my future. One thing was very clear. Paoli had nothing to offer me. They already had a town drunk. It was starting to look like going back in the Navy was my only option. I considered the Marines or the Army, but I decided I couldn't start over again at the bottom of the ranks. I talked to the Navy recruiter, and he was trying again to get me a deal where I could change my job but keep my rank (E-6).

While he was working on that, I saw an ad in a newspaper for overseas construction jobs. There was a company in Indianapolis, so I decided to go there to see what they had to offer. I borrowed eight hundred dollars from the bank, and got on a bus to Indianapolis. Old habits die hard.

When I got to Indianapolis, I got a room in a cheap hotel and went to a bar. I was going to the construction office the next day. Three days later I was broke and hitchhiking my way back to Paoli. I'm not sure what all happened in that three day period, but I never made it to the office. I guess the only good thing was I never made it to jail either. So again I was back in Paoli, but this time I could add being eight hundred dollars in debt to my list of problems.

It appeared I would be going back in the Navy—deal or no deal. It was depressing to think that the only thing I was good for was being a drunken sailor. Before I signed up again, I happened to run into a girl I used to date. She was three or four years younger than I, and she was now a schoolteacher. We went on a couple of dates, and I told her I'd be leaving again soon for the Navy. She told me I should go back to school. I told her I was too old to go back to school. I'd be thirty before I graduated. She said, "You've got your whole life ahead of you. How old are you going to be if you don't do it?" I thought about what she'd said, and I called the Pharmacy School at Purdue to find out if I could get back into school. It was about three weeks until the summer session began. I set up an interview with one of the school professors. Then I had to figure out how to get to the interview since I still didn't have a driver's license.

My sister agreed to take me, but her car was being worked on, so we had to take my father's car. His car wasn't in good shape either, and it stopped on us about halfway there. We managed to get it started again, and we finally made it to Purdue. In the seven years I had been gone, the campus had changed quite a bit. We went to the building I thought was the pharmacy school, and found out that the school had moved to a new building a couple of years earlier. Things just kept getting better. My interview was with a professor and I was late.

When we entered the offices, there was a woman about my age standing just inside the door. I told her I had an interview with this professor, and could she tell me where to find his office. She said, "Sure—follow me." She took me to an office, went and sat behind the desk, smiled and said, "What can I do for you?" It turned out she was very nice, and she told me I could get back into the school, but she wanted me to take a couple of classes that summer to prove to her I could do it. So she signed me up for organic chemistry and physics. She also told me that the look on my face when she told me who she was had made her day!

So I was going to be a college student again. Makes perfect sense doesn't it? A twenty-seven year old drunken sailor who's been in several jails, mental wards, has a vocabulary that consists of many variations of the word fuck, and whose main talent is bar fighting should breeze right through organic chemistry and physics. No problem there. After leaving the school we got a newspaper and starting looking for a place for me to live. I found a three-room apartment close to campus and the town. The whole place was about the size of my bathroom and closet in my present house. The rent was $145 per month plus utilities. My GI Bill was going to be only $175 each month, so that wouldn't leave much for minor luxuries like food. We managed to get back home without the car breaking down. Now I had to figure out how I was going to pull off this change of life.

Many people will tell you that money doesn't matter in life. These are people who have never been totally broke. I was signed up for summer classes at Purdue. How the hell was I going to pay for it? Not only was I broke, but I was eight hundred dollars in debt. I couldn't get a student loan because of the money I owed. I needed money for the tuition, books, rent, and food. So basically I was screwed. I told my dad that I was going back to Navy. I didn't have any choice since I couldn't get the money for school. He didn't say much. He went down to the basement, and came back with a roll of musty twenty dollar bills. He handed me the money.

"What's this for?"

"I think going back into the Navy would probably be the best for you. If you don't change yourself even that won't work out for you. If you seriously want to try school, this will at least give you a chance. It'll probably be your last chance, so you better not blow it."

"I'm going to do my best. You know I'm probably not going to be able to pay you back. I promise I'll try not to waste it."

He had given me eight hundred dollars in cash. I paid off the loan, and then I was able to get a student loan and money from the GI Bill to go to school. Why did he do that? That was a lot of money for him, and I had never done anything to deserve it. So whatever you think about the importance of money in life, I can tell you that eight hundred dollars made it possible for me to change my life. Now when I give money to someone to help them get through some crisis or another, even if I think it will probably not change anything, I know that at least it might give them a chance. Sometimes a chance is all you need. I can get more money. They might not get another chance.

The apartment was furnished, if you could call it that. I had a bed and a chair, and my family gave me a few cooking utensils (although I never had anything to cook), some bedding, and towels. Besides a few clothes left over from high school, moving in wasn't a very involved process. My sister took me back on the Wednesday of the week before classes started. My dad gave me money for the rent until the checks from the GI Bill started. I gave the landlord the rent for two months, and bought a few food items and the books I needed.

So did I start readjusting my thinking to get ready for school? Of course not. I went to a bar. You should be able to guess what happened next. You're right. I got drunk, got into a fight, and was thrown into jail. The war in Vietnam was not popular at that time, and a few of the drunks at the bar expressed their feelings about us "baby killers." So I quietly explained to them that I had friends killed there, and still had friends in harm's way, and on their behalf I felt that I should express their thoughts as they would if they were here. Then I stomped the shit out of several of the peace-loving assholes.

One of the cops was a Vietnam vet, and after they locked me up, he came and talked to me. He gave me one of his cards, told me the name of the prosecutor, and told me to go to see the guy before court started. He said to give him his card, tell him the truth, and he would probably give me a break. This was Wednesday, and I was scheduled for court Friday morning. He said he'd call the prosecutor before Friday. They were holding me on a $250 bond, so I only needed twenty-five dollars to bail me out. The problem was I didn't know anyone there to call. I found my landlord's card in my pocket, so I called him.

"Mr. Ellis, this is Mike Webster. I'm the person you rented an apartment to last week. I'm sorry to bother you, but I need some help and you're the only person I know in town."

"I remember you. Aren't you the one who just got out of the Navy? What kind of help do you need? I'll help if I can."

"I'm ashamed I have to tell you this, but I'm in jail. I got into a bar fight and got locked up. I need someone to bail me out. The bail's only twenty-five dollars, but I don't have any money on me. I got some at the apartment, so I can pay you back. I'll understand if you say no."

"Well, I got to admit I wasn't expecting this." There was silence for a moment. "I'll try to come and get you in a couple of hours."

Believe it or not he came and bailed me out. He took me back to the apartment, and I gave him his twenty-five dollars back, and promised him I would never repeat this stupid episode. He said he'd had problems in his past, and if I needed anything I could call him. Again I was being treated with more respect than I deserved by him and the cop.

So on Friday morning I went to the court house, found the prosecutor, and did as the cop had told me. He put me first on the docket. He told me if I would plead guilty and assure him he'd never see me again, he would recommend that the judge dismiss the charge. I did as he said, and once again I was given another chance. I spent the weekend doing nothing but thinking about how I was really going to wind up. I had serious doubts I would ever be a normal person again. I knew that sooner or later my luck was going to run out. I decided I would make myself at least try one more time. I would do the best I could to make it through summer school. If I couldn't do it, I would go back to the Navy.

It was weird being a college student again. The classes were smaller since it was summer school. I was sort of a curious oddity to the other students. Some wanted to know what was really going on in Vietnam. All they knew about it was what they saw every night on television news. I tried to explain to them that no matter why the war was happening, the guys fighting it were trying to keep themselves and their friends alive. Most were amazed that I volunteered to go there, and that I would go back if I could. There was another "old guy" in my chemistry class. He was married and had three kids. He and I became good friends and as it turned out later, he would be the best man at my wedding.

The classes were hard, but I found it was easier to study now that I was older. I aced the first exam in chemistry, but I got a twenty-seven percent on the first physics exam, and there were nine others below me! They all dropped the class. I couldn't do that. This was the "make it or break it" time in my life. The first time I was in school here, physics was the only class I'd ever flunked in my life. Even though I felt bad that I flunked a course, back then it was just a bad grade. Now it was the most important grade of my life. If I flunked, or even got a low grade, I would not get back into pharmacy school. That would leave me with only one choice. I would be going back into the Navy and back to being just another drunken dumbass. It was definitely serious. I decided I was not going to give up without a fight.

I went to the bookstore and got a book on working physics problems. I don't remember the title, but it was something like *Physics for Dumbasses*. I spent the whole weekend doing nothing but working physics problems. The grad student teaching assistant was a pretty good-looking girl around twenty-four years old. She had been pretty friendly, and even flirted with me. I decided to go to her for help. After a couple of coffee dates, I persuaded her to give me a makeup test to replace that grade. I got a ninety-three percent on the make up exam. From that point on physics was not a problem for me. I got a B in the course. In the chemistry class I had the highest average in the class (eighty-nine percent), but ninety percent was an A, so I wound up with a B in that course as well. Now I know getting a couple of B's might not seem like such a big deal to you. For me, however, it was a very big deal. It gave me a new start in life when I was twenty-seven years old. All in all, it wasn't a bad showing for a drunken sailor. I bought some sunglasses. My future was looking a little brighter!

Starting Over—From the Middle

So there I was, a full-time college student again. It had only taken me nine years to start the third year of pharmacy school. I took as many hours as I could. I figured I could finish the remaining three years in two and a half if I carried the maximum hours each semester and went to summer school again.

I noticed a big difference between this class and the one I left seven years ago. That class was small and only had twelve women in it. This one was larger and almost half women. Even though I did all right in the summer session, it was evident right from the start I was going to spend most of my time studying. That didn't prove to be a problem. My attitude was different now. I knew I had to make it through or wind up back in the Navy.

There were a couple of habits I had to break. The first was communicating with people without using some variation of the word fuck. After seven years of using it constantly, I had to really concentrate before I spoke to anyone. When you're ordering sailors to do something, being nice with polite speech doesn't get the job done. For instance, if I wanted someone to wake up and fix a problem he had caused, I wouldn't gently shake him and say, "Wake up! You've got to go to the engine room and fix that leaking water line like I told you to do before." He would just turn over and go back to sleep. However, if I grabbed and shook him and said (loudly), "*Wake the fuck up asshole! Are you tired? I don't give a flying fuck!* You've got *thirty fucking seconds to get your skinny fucking ass* to the engine room and fix that leak like you were told to do. *Do you fucking understand me fuckhead?*" The chances are much better that he'd fix the leak.

The other habit was much harder to break. I had this really bad habit of wanting to eat every day. Since I had very little money to buy food, this made me become creative with diet planning. Every week I'd have to figure out what to buy that I could ration out so at least I ate something every day. A can of Campbell's Tomato Soup only cost a dime, so some weeks I had a can of soup a day. I found a package of bacon and a carton of eggs would last almost a week if I had two eggs and two or three pieces of bacon a day. One week I bought only a gallon of milk and had a glass of milk a day. This technically wasn't eating, but it worked. Popcorn was cheap, and it fills you up, so I'd eat popcorn daily for a week.

There was a men's co-op next to my apartment, and one night I "liberated" a very large jar of peanut butter from them. The peanut butter lasted a long time, and I only had to buy a loaf of bread and a jar of jelly. Yes, I know it was stealing. It bothered me but I promised myself I'd make up for it someday. Years later, a pharmacy technician told me that a homeless man was stealing food from his fraternity house. He knew I was a martial artist and asked me what they should do. I told him to station a watch around the clock until they caught the guy. Then they should take him out and buy him a good meal. I don't think it was the answer he expected from me.

A couple of times I sold a pint of blood for five dollars. The last time I tried to do that they wouldn't do it because I was so run down. A nurse felt sorry for me and gave me five dollars. That bothered me too, but I took it and put another thing on my list to repay some day. I think I've paid those debts. I hope so. Sometimes when I give people money to buy food, others tell me I'm being scammed. That may be so, but the people telling me this haven't ever been really hungry. Although

I don't recommend it, poverty is a great way to diet. I lost sixty-five pounds that year.

Since I was studying all the time and had no money, I didn't have much of a social life. My buddy from summer school and a couple of girls who were also pharmacy students were the only people I hung out with very much. One of the girls was from southern Indiana, so we had that in common. The other girl was in the summer school organic chemistry class with my buddy and me, and we studied together a lot. She took notes in class better than anyone I have ever seen. She wrote down almost every word the professor said. She heard things the rest of us had missed. We'd copy her notes all the time. Sometimes that was better than going to the lecture.

Sometimes my friend and I would cut the lecture and just get her notes. I can't remember what class it was, but I remember the first time we left the lecture while the class was going. We were in a big lecture hall, and he and I were about ten rows from the front. The guy lecturing was boring as hell, and about half way through the hour he said, "Why don't we go and get a Coke? We can get her notes later."

"You just want to get up in middle of the lecture and leave?"

"They don't take roll. This guy is putting me asleep."

So we got up and slowly walked all the way up the center aisle to the doors at the back. All the way up the stairs, we could hear people whispering. They were wondering what the hell we were doing. They were all waiting for the professor to say something to us, but as far as I can remember he never even seemed to notice us. Later that day some of the others told us they couldn't believe we had the guts to just walk out!

We stayed through the whole period for the next few lectures, but a couple of weeks later we decided to leave again. This time as we were going up the stairs, I didn't hear whispering, but I heard noise behind us. I looked back and about a third of the class was following us up the stairs! After that we stayed the whole period if we went, but we cut that lecture on a regular basis, along with a lot of other students.

The semester went quickly, and I finished with a B average in all the classes. I had proven to myself that I could make it if I applied myself. It renewed my determination to change. My life wasn't very exciting, but it was the longest time I had been straight in the last seven years.

Unfortunately it wasn't because of my will, but being broke that kept me out of the bars. In any case, it was a good start.

Shortly after the second semester started, I noticed a girl who was always sitting a row or two in front of me in every lecture since we were seated in alphabetical order in all our pharmacy classes. I thought she was beautiful, but I was curious about her unconventional looks. She had red hair, and it was real kinky and in an Afro style. I wondered how she got her hair that way. I thought she might be half black, but she really didn't look like it. I remember asking the other girls if they thought she fixed her hair that way on purpose, but I can't remember what they said. Anyway, it intrigued me, and I looked up her name on the seating chart.

Her name was Margaret Stahlhut. This confused me further, because I was sure I had heard someone call her Peggy. I didn't know Peggy was a nickname for Margaret. Another thing I noticed was her shoes. She was sitting across from me in a lab, and her shoes looked odd to me. They were kind of heavy and squared off at the toes. Of course I had no idea what was in style in women's shoes. I thought, poor girl, she has kinky hair and deformed feet. But regardless of this she was attractive and she fascinated me.

I wanted to talk to her, but I really didn't know how to approach her. We were getting back an exam in lab, so I had an idea. I noticed she generally made higher scores than I did. I'd use that to break the ice.

"How do you think you did on this test?"

"I probably did okay. I didn't think it was that hard."

"I've noticed that you usually beat me, but I studied more for this one. I'll bet you a Coke that I beat you this time." If she made the bet, I was going to win either way. She thought about it for a minute. I didn't think she was going for it.

"I really didn't study that much, but I guess I can afford a Coke. I'll bet you."

I really wasn't surprised when I lost. I was pretty sure I was going to.

"I guess I didn't study enough. I really thought I'd win this one. Seems I owe you a Coke. This is my last class today. What about you?

If you've got the time, we could go the Union and you can collect your winnings."

"I guess I'm done for the day. I don't have anything to do for a couple of hours."

So we went to the Union. On the way there it occurred to me I might not have enough money on me for two Cokes. We got a booth, and when I went to get the drinks I was wondering what I was going to do if I didn't have enough to pay for them. Luckily I had barely enough. I didn't have to be embarrassed to go back to the booth. Now what would I talk about?

"I know you're smart. I suppose you've figured out that the bet was a win-win situation for me either way. I just wanted to meet you."

"Yeah, I knew it."

"Can I ask you a question? I'd like to know something about you, but I don't want to make you mad."

"I doubt if I'll get mad. What do you want to know?"

"Do you do your hair that way, or is it natural?"

"It's natural. All I do is wash it, and it comes out this way. I used to straighten it, but it was too much trouble. I can tame it with rollers but I enjoy the freedom and uniqueness."

"I suppose you don't have deformed feet either."

"What makes you think that?" She started laughing.

"Your shoes look like they're cut short with the toes cut off."

"No, I don't think I have deformed feet. I think they're pretty normal."

So I found out that her feet and hair were normal.

Even though I wouldn't eat for a while if I used my food money, I asked her if she wanted to go see a movie with me. *The Godfather* was just opening at a movie in town. I had read the book, and I told her I thought it'd be a good movie. To my surprise she accepted. Now I had to tell her I didn't have a car, so I guess we'd have to take the local bus to town. She said she had a car. It was VW Beetle, and we could use it. She said I could drive if I wanted, so I had to tell her I didn't have a license. I don't think I told her why.

It was a good movie, but if you had read the book it was easier to know what was happening. About half the people in the theater were whispering to the others who hadn't read the book, explaining the movie to them. After the movie we went to Bruno's Pizza. It was the best pizza around. It was a good date. I can still remember what she was wearing—a short black and white checkered skirt and a black top. It was nice to be talking to a normal girl instead of some bar girl. I found out several interesting things about her and her family. She was from Lincoln, Illinois. She had three sisters—two older and one younger than her. Her father was a hospital administrator. He was also a friend of one of the professors at the pharmacy school. That's how she wound up coming to Purdue. She was actually a high school dropout. She had quit high school when she was sixteen and went to college. It was obvious that she was smarter than I, and her life was definitely different than mine had been.

Her roommate warned her about going out with an ex-sailor with a tattoo, but Peggy and I continued to hang out together. The first time she came to my apartment I don't think she was too impressed with my "luxury" living conditions. All I had in my refrigerator was a jar of mayonnaise, some ketchup packets, and water. I used the ketchup to make "tomato soup." Despite this, we started spending a lot of time together, and she became an addition to our study group. After studying with her, my grades got better. The semester went pretty fast, and I survived again with a B average overall.

I can't remember what Peggy was going to do that summer, but when she was leaving to go home we were arguing about something. When she came to get some of her stuff from my apartment, she just stuffed things in a bag and left without saying much. As soon as she left, I discovered she'd taken all of the towels. I yelled out the window, "You took all my towels!" When she brought back the towels we talked some more, and things were better between us when she left. If she hadn't taken the towels, our lives may have turned out differently.

I was going to go to the first session of summer school, and then go and work in a pharmacy in my hometown. I left that apartment, and moved in with three other guys for the summer session. I took a couple of easy courses just to get the hours. Peggy and I wrote and I called her a few times. I aced the courses and went home to work for the rest of the summer. It was strange to be living at home again. Since I was working, I paid my parents some rent. It was also very strange to be eating regularly again.

I had never even been in a pharmacy before, and the day I started the owner said he was glad I was there, gave me the keys, and said he'd see me in a couple of weeks.

"What do you mean in a couple of weeks? Where are you going?"

"We're going on vacation. We haven't been on one for three years."

"You're just going to leave me here? I've never filled a prescription before. I've never even set foot in a pharmacy."

"You'll be fine. Bob and Martha will help you out," he said. He explained that Louie, the previous owner, would be in the office so I'd be legal.

With that he left on his vacation. Louie was around eighty years old. He had kept his license, but he hadn't practiced in twenty years. Most of the time he sat in the office and slept. Bob and Martha had technician licenses, and they filled most of the prescriptions. Every now and then I'd have them go check to make sure our supervising pharmacist was still breathing. The law says a licensed pharmacist has to be there—it doesn't specify that he has to be alive! Both of them had been working there for a long time, so they knew what they were doing.

One day Bob came running to the pharmacy shouting, "White lotion! White lotion!" I had no idea what was happening. "White lotion" was a warning code that the Pharmacy Inspector was coming. It so happens that the pharmacy inspector was a retired state police officer who lived in Paoli. So I'm sure he was aware of what was going on there. He was a nice guy, and when he was in the state police he had helped several people in town out of tough spots. I was one of them. The summer before I went into the Navy, I found out that my old friends, the twins from Pennsylvania, were living in Evansville, Indiana, which is about one hundred miles from Paoli. They had been in a car wreck. A truck ran a red light and hit their car. They both went through the windshield and walked to the hospital—they were tough guys! I wanted to go visit them so I borrowed my dad's '59 Oldsmobile and drove to Evansville. They looked pretty beat-up, but it didn't stop them from drinking.

We drank a lot of beer and talked over old times. I was drunk when I left them, and since it was a Saturday night, I stopped at a dance place in Jasper, Indiana, on the way home. I was totally bombed when I left there, and my luck finally ran out. I missed a curve. I took out a telephone pole, a mailbox, a guy's driveway, and the front porch off his house. Then I kept on going! I wound up back on the road, and I continued to Paoli. I really didn't know what I had hit.

Back in Paoli I went to an all-night restaurant. When I got out and looked at the car, I couldn't believe the damage. There was not a part of the car that wasn't totally demolished. So I did what any dumbass drunk would do. I drove all the way back to Evansville to show the twins. All the way back I kept looking for what I'd hit, but my drunken eyes never saw anything. They couldn't believe what I'd done. After I'd been there long enough to sober up, I went back to Paoli.

When I pulled into the driveway there was a state police car sitting there waiting for me. It was the officer that lived in town. When he told me what I'd hit, I couldn't believe the car was still running and I was still alive. He said I couldn't have done any more damage if I'd been driving a tank. A car that I'd run off the road had followed me and taken down my license number. When the town cops had called him, he told them he'd take care of it.

After he had finished telling me what a dumbass I was, he told me to go see a justice of the peace in Jasper the next day. He said he'd call him and tell him I was coming. I don't remember how I got there, but I did as I was told. The justice of the peace told me that as a favor to the state police officer, if I pleaded guilty to leaving the scene of an accident, he would drop all of the other charges against me. So instead of being locked up forever as I should have been, I paid a one hundred dollar fine. A few days later I joined the Navy.

So the pharmacy inspector was no stranger to me. In fact, the reason he had come to the pharmacy was to see me.

"How are you doing Mike? You haven't been driving through anyone's house lately, have you? If I remember right, the last guy wasn't too happy with your remodeling job."

"I hope my house remodeling days are gone forever. I never got to thank you for helping me out then. I know you did me a big favor. I'm going to do my best to not make you sorry that you did it."

"I'm glad to see you're heading the right direction. Keep up the good work. Oh, and by the way, don't get any of that white lotion on you." Then he left the store laughing. I never saw him again until I was taking the pharmacy boards.

Peggy came to Paoli to visit that summer, and we spent a good weekend in Louisville. When she left I thought we were back together, but I soon got a letter that was basically a breakup letter. I didn't know what had changed, but I wrote back and told her I hoped she had a happy life even if it didn't include me.

That summer I met a schoolteacher who was a friend of the pharmacy owner, so I started to date her. I seemed to have a thing with schoolteachers. We spent a lot of time together, and when I went back to school she wrote to me almost every day.

I had gotten my driver's license back and bought a car. It was a '65 Chevelle in great shape. I found another apartment close to campus, and started my fourth year with a full course load. Of course, I saw Peggy in about every class. It wasn't long until we got back together. Then I had to write the breakup letter to the school teacher. I never saw or heard from her again.

Peggy eventually moved in with me, and we got married on New Year's Eve that year. She was only twenty years old, and I was an old fart of twenty-nine. I'll admit that I was nervous as hell, and I wasn't the only one. During the ceremony, Peggy was hyperventilating and almost passed out. It was probably the best decision I had ever made. Unfortunately, my dark side was still with me. It would now affect Peggy as well. Over the years she would stick by me when she should have left. That's the only reason I'm still here writing this.

After we were married, our financial situation became much better. Peggy's father gave her some oil company stocks and my GI Bill payment increased. The second semester of the fourth year went quickly, and we both did well in all the classes. Since we weren't hurting for money, we spent the summer on vacation. It was the first summer in a long time that I didn't work or go to school. I had enough hours so I would be able to graduate after the first semester of our fifth year. Peggy was going to spend the last semester doing internships.

Working as a pharmacy apprentice in Paoli (1972).

Real World Experience

I graduated in December of 1973. It had only taken me twelve years to get through five years of pharmacy school. Our friend helped get me a job at an independent pharmacy in her hometown Washington, Indiana. It was a busy pharmacy owned by two guys. We went there on a weekend before I graduated so I could check out the place and finalize my employment. We checked into a motel around 5:30 PM on a Friday night, and I went to the store to find out what time I was supposed to start Saturday morning. As soon as I walked into the pharmacy, one of the owners gave me a handful of prescription bottles and said, "Get busy." By the time the store closed at 8 PM, I had filled more prescriptions than I had ever seen until then. I went back to the motel and told Peggy that I was pretty sure I had made a mistake by taking this job. By the time Saturday was over, I was sure of it. I was pretty much stuck with it. If I wasn't a dumbass, I would have checked before I took the job. Even worse, I never learned from that mistake. In the future I would make the same mistake again.

We had already found a place to live in Vincennes, Indiana, and Peggy was going to do her internship at a pharmacy there. So in January of '74 I got my introduction to the real world of pharmacy. We filled around eight hundred prescriptions a day, and that was without the use of computers. It was a fast paced, high stress job. One of the owners was a nice guy. The other one was as big an asshole as I had ever seen. He always had one or another of the female employees crying. He pissed me off so much my stomach hurt when I got home at night. I won't go into all the different things we did. You'd have to be a pharmacist to fully appreciate them. Just believe me when I say we bent many laws, and all that mattered to them was making money. The store was doing around a million dollars a year. That was really a lot of money then. They were paying me a high salary, but I earned every penny of it. I turned down the offer to work there after getting licensed.

Peggy graduated in May of 1974. We both took jobs with Hook's Drugs, which was the largest chain in Indiana at that time. We moved to Marion, Indiana, and Peggy worked in a new store there. The store I went to was in Gas City, a few miles from Marion. We were pharmacists, but we couldn't work alone until we passed the board and were registered. The boards were given at Purdue. It was going to be three days of total stress. Not passing meant you had wasted five years of your life for basically nothing. You would have to wait until the test was given again, and you only got three chances to pass. The test was divided up into different sections, and if you flunked any section, you flunked it all. We studied when we weren't working, but there were a lot of things that we hadn't reviewed in years. I was definitely concerned, because it had been a lot longer for me since I took a seven-year break.

The first part of the test was calculations. It was a multiple choice test, but they had worked the problems every way you could do them wrong, so no matter how you did the problem, you would get an answer that matched one of the choices. Remember, we didn't have calculators then. When we went back to the motel that night and compared notes, it seemed we had gotten different answers on every problem we remembered. Since Peggy was smarter than me, I thought I had flunked the test on the first section. Each night was the same. We had different answers on many of the questions. Every section was hard! The law section was really bad. One of the proctors giving the test was the state inspector from my home town. He kept coming by and looking over my shoulder to see how I was doing. He actually tried to help me on a question, but he didn't know the answer either. I thought it was really a badly-written test if the person that enforces the law couldn't answer the questions.

It was a long three days. Waiting for the scores took quite a while, and that didn't help my nerves any. Opening the letter was a tense time. I had passed! I don't remember the score, but it was in the high 80s. Peggy had the highest score of the whole test, which I thought was impressive, since over two hundred people had taken the test.

The store I was working at was a new store, but they had bought out an independent pharmacy so the store was busier than the one in Marion. The hours were 9 AM to 10 PM on Monday through Saturday and 9 AM to 9 PM on Sundays and holidays. That's something they don't tell you in pharmacy school. How you get to work thirteen hour days with no meal or break times. We didn't get overtime pay since we were management and on salary. The pharmacist they bought out was sixty-four years old, and they made him the manager of the store. They told me that they wanted me to get to know all of the customers, because Hook's had mandatory retirement at sixty-five, and I would take over as manager when he retired. So I did just that. I got to know the people and the local doctors. Then he got sick, and I worked ninety hour weeks for several weeks. He came back to work a couple of weeks before his 65th birthday. When he turned sixty-five he didn't retire. When I asked the company what happened to the mandatory retirement, they said they were going to let him work. He just wouldn't have any benefits. So I quit and took a job with Haag's Drugs in Marion. They had twelve hour days and ten hour Sundays and holidays. Hook's management flew down to Gas City in a helicopter to try to talk me out of leaving. I told them no thanks. I'd been screwed enough and I was moving on.

I'd only been at Haag's a couple of months when my father died. He drove himself to the hospital and died a couple of days later. I was at work when my sister called to tell me. I think surprise was my first reaction. He hardly ever went to the doctor, and since we didn't talk that much, I never thought he was in bad health. I knew my mother had heart problems, and I thought she would die before him. I never got to totally repay him for saving my ass. I can't say I really knew that much about him. In fact, there was a time in my life I wondered if he was really my father.

When I was young, mom took me to the movies every Saturday night. I was always running around like any kid, but I noticed that mom always sat beside the same man in the back row every time. When I became an adult it entered my mind occasionally that something had been going on, but it never really bothered me. After all, my father was forty and my mom was thirty-seven when I was born. I can't really think that they wanted another child at that time of their lives. I can't remember ever having an actual conversation with him. Forty is a large generation gap to overcome. The truth is not important. Even if he never displayed much emotion toward me, he was there when I needed help. Since I had destroyed his house and two of his cars, I'd say he gave me a lot more respect than I deserved. He liked Peggy. He must have known she was going to be good for me. He actually went to the store and bought her a Christmas present. It was a silver makeup mirror. As far as I know, he had never done that for anyone else in the family.

We had plenty of money now. We just didn't have much free time to enjoy it. I did find time to do two things. I bought a new Corvette and started taking flying lessons. I almost bought a new airplane. I soloed after six hours, but I never felt that comfortable about it. My instructor kept telling me how good I was doing, but I never felt I was in total control of the plane. Also, I was not in total control of my life. I still had times when I reverted to being a sailor, but I was lucky and never had any really bad episodes. Peggy wanted to move to Illinois to be closer to her family. It really didn't matter to me, so we both quit our jobs and went to Illinois. After we were licensed, I took a job with an independent pharmacy in Washington, Illinois. I made the same dumbass mistake not checking out the job better.

We moved there, and I started work on a Sunday morning from 9 AM to 1 PM. It wasn't as bad as my last job with an independent, but I could tell it was going to be bad. I went to work on Monday, and by the end of the day I knew it wasn't going to work out. I told Peggy I was sorry, but I just couldn't handle it. Even though we had moved, and she didn't have a job, I wasn't going to work there. So I called the owner and told him I had to quit. He said I had done so well, and that I would fit right in there. I told him yes, I could do it, but I was not going to work in another crazily-run pharmacy. Here we were all moved in and out of work. I'm sure Peggy was sorry she hadn't listened to her roommate. She shouldn't have gotten mixed up with an ex-sailor with a tattoo.

I was only out of work for a couple of weeks. I took a job at a Super-X in Bartonville, Illinois, about twenty miles from Washington. It wasn't that bad of a job, but I wound up working long hours and drinking again. I liked several of the employees, and they weren't as bad as sailors, but they all drank quite a bit. Since I still didn't have control of my life, I was drinking just because everyone else did. I met Larry, the husband of one of the employees. He was a cop in Bartonville, and he and I became friends. He was also an alcoholic. Peggy wasn't working, and I was either working or partying, so things weren't that great with us. One night after work I went and had a few drinks. On the way home a truck pulled out in front of me without his lights on and I hit him. It took about half the front of the Corvette off. As soon as I got out of the car the driver and the guy with him jumped out.

The passenger said, "I told you to turn your lights on." Of course, when the cop got there, they both lied about it and I had been drinking, so I was screwed. It was a Peoria cop, but I thought I had one chance to get out of this. When he got me in the car, I told him my friend was on the job in Bartonville, and if he'd call him he'd come and take care of me. I told him the Corvette was screwed up, and if he busted me for a DUI my life would be down the drain. It took a lot of talking, but I convinced him to take me to Larry's house in Bartonville. Luckily he was home, and he got me released to him. Once again I'd talked my way out of deep shit. You'd think by now I would be smart enough to know my luck was running out. Unfortunately, I hadn't hit bottom yet, but it was not far off.

I saw an ad in the newspaper for a pharmacy for sale in Glasford, Illinois. It was a small town about twenty-five miles from Peoria. I went to look at it, and it seemed to be a nice little store. After talking to the owner and the town's bank president, I basically went home that night and told Peggy, "I bought a pharmacy. You're going to work there tomorrow." Needless to say, she was quite surprised. She should have left then and taken all the towels. But the next day she went to

Glasford to see her new pharmacy. The town bank loaned us the money using the farm in Indiana for collateral. Since the Corvette was out of commission, I bought an old car to drive to work and back. Peggy found us an apartment in Glasford. When I asked if it was close to the pharmacy, she said it was right across the street. She wasn't kidding. It was on the other side of Main Street about a hundred feet from the store. You would think that would be a good thing, but living there would lead to another major blowup in my life.

Gunfight at the IGA

When I bought the pharmacy in Glasford, I had been working long hours at the Super-X. The other pharmacist there had left, and again I was stuck working the pharmacy by myself. After a couple of months, I had enough. I got drunk and quit my job. My drunken mind said, "You own a pharmacy. Why are you working your ass off for Super-X?" If I had been sober, I would have known that my pharmacy wouldn't make enough to cover the salary I'd lose by quitting.

Unfortunately the dumbass drunk me had already quit, so I was going to have to make it work. At least I wouldn't be spending money on gas driving to work. Our apartment was only about one hundred feet from the store on the other side of the street. The store was on a street corner. On the other two corners there was an IGA grocery store on the same side, and a bar was directly across from the store. Since the apartment was two doors down from the bar, drunks were always trying to come in our door thinking it was the bar. This was not a good thing, but it was the parking lot of the grocery store that proved to be the real problem.

I discovered that the IGA parking lot was the party place for every drunk and doper in the county. Almost every night it was full. Some nights the party went full blast until daybreak. They must have had scanners, because if the county sheriff was called, the lot would empty out until the sheriff left town. I put an alarm system in the pharmacy, but I couldn't ignore the loud partying every night. My friend Larry got me a .38 pistol and a police riot shotgun. It wasn't long before the store was broken into. They kicked in the glass door, and then ran through the pharmacy grabbing drugs. They were gone before the county sheriff arrived. I decided then that I would have to be the first to respond to the alarm, or this was never going to stop.

About a week later the same guy kicked in the door again. This time the sheriff had a tip that he was going to do it. They staked out the store and watched him do it. They were waiting for him when he came out. They had him in handcuffs when I got there with the shotgun. They probably saved his life. The next day one of the local dopers was in the store mouthing off about something. I ran him out of the store and he kept saying something about how nobody could stop them from doing whatever they wanted. I told him six shots from a .38 might slow him down. He said, "I'm not scared of guns." That statement proved to be not entirely true.

Everyone in town knew what was going on every night. One old lady told me she thought someone should get up on the roof of the IGA with a shotgun. She said, "I'd do it if I could." When I asked why the town didn't stop it, I never got a definite answer. I even went to a town meeting, and they basically said there was nothing they could do. I asked why they didn't hire an off duty cop to work at least part-time? They told me the town couldn't afford it. So basically the doper had been right. They could do whatever they wanted.

Within the next two weeks they proved it. They painted on my building and several others, broke the bank's sign, broke the window in the telephone office, tore the letters off the front of the post office, damaged gas pumps at the gas station, and dug up or drove over all the flowers a women's club had planted along Main Street. The partying never slowed down. I talked to the mayor again. He said nothing could be done. He did say that they had hired a part-time cop who would work a couple of nights a week, but he didn't think anyone could clear that parking lot. You know what? He was wrong. A couple of nights later I came back from Bartonville where I had been drinking with Larry. When I went past the parking lot it was full, and someone yelled something at me. That did it. I parked the car and went to clear the parking lot. There must have been thirty or more people there. They overpowered me, and I told them they were right that nobody could clear them out. They let me go, and I went home and got the shotgun. It was loaded with deer slugs and OO buckshot. Right before I set foot in the lot, I fired a shot in the air. Before the echo of the shot had died down, cars were starting and they were running over each other trying to get out. It was like cockroaches when you turn the light on. The brave tough guy I had thrown out of my store had three guys in his backseat and a passenger in the front. They were all screaming at him to go, but he was shaking so badly he couldn't get the key in the ignition. I pressed the barrel of the shotgun into his left ear and said, "What's the matter? Change your mind about not being scared of guns?" He had gotten the key in, but he couldn't get it started. His passengers bailed on him and ran.

It was then I heard someone shout, "Lower the weapon or I'll shoot!" I looked to the left and there was a police car. The cop was behind his door and had his gun on me. The part-time cop was having an exciting first night of work. He told me again to lower the weapon. I was sober enough to lay the shotgun on the ground. The doper finally got his car started and peeled out of the lot. There was nobody on Main Street but me and the cop. He asked, "What the hell's going on?"

I told him, "They said this parking lot couldn't be cleared. I think I proved them wrong. I think it's pretty well cleared, don't you?" About that time the county cops arrived. I told them all what had happened. The county cops told me to go home. The new town cop became full-time after that night. It turned out he was a retired Navy first class. He and I became good friends.

Since the town now had a cop, and every doper in the county had to find a new hangout, you would think all of those people who complained would be happy and grateful to me for bringing it about. As you can imagine, I was definitely the hot gossip all around town. It was not what you would expect, however. I was being portrayed as a drunken madman who had attacked innocent children. These churchgoing model citizen teenagers were just sitting around talking about sports and school, and suddenly they were attacked for no reason. And now there's a cop around all the time and is that really necessary?

I admit the town's reaction was surprising to me. My cop friends were not surprised. They told me that nobody wants a cop around until someone shits on their front porch. I now know that is definitely true. The tough guy's parents lead the movement to get me locked up. Seems I scared their poor innocent son so badly he couldn't even go out on his own to look for a job. They succeeded in getting a grand jury to consider charges for "attempted murder" and "assault with a deadly weapon." To get the indictment, they had to prove I had pointed the gun at him. All of the cops testified that they never saw me actually point the weapon at him. Their testimony won out over his. So just like O.J., I was innocent.

They still filed some lesser charges, and after two or three months of the case being postponed, the town cop and I went to see the prosecutor. I suggested a plea bargain, and he accepted it. I pleaded guilty to "discharging a firearm within city limits." I was sentenced to one day in jail, probation for one year with the records expunged at that time, and the shotgun was confiscated. I persuaded the judge to give it to the Glasford police department. So one Sunday I spent twelve hours in the Peoria jail.

That pretty much ended it, but Glasford and I were done too. As far as I was concerned, if I saw someone burning the town down I'd just look the other way. It was not completely over, though. I got a letter from the Illinois Pharmacy Board. I had to go to Chicago and explain it all over again. After showing them the pictures of the damage in town, and telling them I tried to do it legally, they too told me not to do it anymore. So now was it over? Not totally. It would come back to bite me on the ass in the future. However, it was a turning point for me. I had hit bottom. It was sheer luck I didn't kill someone that night. If that gun had gone off, it would have taken the driver's and the passenger's head off. I was thirty-three years old. It was time to grow up. The drinking had to stop. Now all I had to do was figure out how to stop it.

125

Awareness—Seeing the Dumbass in the Mirror

Y ou would think any person with even average intelligence would know when their life had bottomed out. I mean how many times do you have to wake up beat-up, bloody, and locked up before you realize your life has turned to shit? Anyone, even a dumbass, should be able to recognize and admit that they have hit bottom. Unfortunately, it's not as simple as it sounds. Homeless shelters, prisons, and graveyards are full of people who failed. For whatever reason, they could not rise from the bottom. It is not a simple thing to change your life. After years of destructive behavior you cannot just decide that you are going to change. If you really try and fail, the depression is unbearable. Death begins to seem preferable to trying and failing again. That's when you have to decide. Live or die. You're finally aware of hitting bottom.

Drugs or alcohol are usually the main reasons your life is in the toilet. I'm sure by now I don't have to tell you my problem was alcohol. I tried going to AA meetings, but I soon figured out that wasn't going to do it for me. If I had to go every day and listen to a bunch of other drunks tell stories, I would rather be dead. I decided that instead of doing something to keep me from drinking, I would have to find something I would rather do than drink. Since I had no other job than my own store, I could arrange a schedule that would allow me to pursue other interests. Flying was the first thing I thought of doing again. Flying made me feel free. It made me concentrate. If I kept my mind on flying, I would not think of drinking.

I checked first at the Peoria airport for a flying school. They had a school, but they flew Cessna planes, which are high wing planes. I learned to fly on Pipers, which are low wing aircraft. I tried a couple of hours in a Cessna 150, but I really didn't like it as well as the Piper Cherokee or Piper Warrior. So I started looking for a school that had Pipers. I found one at a small airport north of Peoria at Mount Hawley. It only had one landing strip, which was a North/South runway. Flying the Pipers was more fun, and I soloed after only a couple of hours in a Warrior. Like the instructor I had before, this one told me how good I was doing. Again like before, I never felt I was doing that great, but I took his word for it. I began thinking I might like to be a flight instructor. It appealed to me a lot more than being a pharmacist.

Becoming a flight instructor gave me a new goal to attain. My mood improved and I spent my spare time studying and flying instead of drinking and fighting. I tried to fly as much as I could to get my basic license. Flying a plane is not that difficult, but landing one is a different story. I was not doing that great judging my flare (stalling and dropping the plane) on landing. I found out why when I took my flight physical. The Navy doctors had been right. My right eye had gotten worse. I had to get glasses for the first time in my life. I had to wear them to drive and fly. It made a big difference in my landings. Having some depth perception stopped the high flares which resulted in no more teeth-jarring landings.

Since landing is difficult, it's something you practice more than anything else. It's called doing touch-and-go's. All you do is land, add power, and take off again. One Sunday it was a beautiful day so I went to the airport to do some touch-and-go's. When I got to the airport, it had become pretty windy. I only had fourteen hours, so I thought it was too windy for me. After watching landings for a while, the wind seemed to be coming straight down the runway, so it didn't seem to be a problem, and I decided to go ahead. It turned out to be another dumbass decision.

I took off easily and continued around the pattern to land. On my final approach the wind was beating the hell out of the plane. It had switched to a gusty crosswind. I was having trouble controlling my approach, and there was a Cessna sitting on the taxiway waiting for me to land so he could take off. I thought I had it under control, but I got too slow and a strong down gust slammed me into the ground a few feet from the end of the runway. I hit the ground *hard*! I heard glass breaking, and the plane bounced up and to the left. I bounced right over the Cessna! I added full power and got it flying right over hangers and other planes tied up at the airport. My left wingtip missed the wind sock by only a few inches. I got back in the landing pattern. I was flying, but my mind was overloaded.

What did I hit? Were my wheels still on? Nobody said a word on the radio, and it never entered my mind to say or ask anything. I continued around the pattern. I was sweating rivers and my left leg was shaking a lot. I decided I had no choice but to land, so I continued. The Cessna wasn't there, and I was ready for the wind this time. When I landed I was surprised that the wheels were still on. I parked the plane and slowly got out. When I looked at the plane I almost had to sit down. There was mud, grass, and clover jammed into the wheel struts, and there was a grass stain on the prop! I took some of the clover flowers out of the struts and went into the terminal. The manager of the airport happened to be a local TV weather man. He was standing at the counter and I laid the flowers down in front of him.

"Where did you get those?" he asked.

"Out of my wheel struts," I said. I can't describe the look on his face. I left him standing there with his mouth open and went into a classroom and sat down.

Even though my hand was shaking badly, I was trying to fill out my logbook.

One of the flight instructors came in and said, "You know you have to go back up."

"No thanks. I've had enough fun for one day," I said.

"You need to go back up now. I'll go with you," he said. I looked at him for a while, and finally said okay. Of course we had to take a different plane, and wait until they cleaned the glass off the runway. The glass was from the runway landing lights. I did nine more landings with no problem.

After the fifth one I told him, "You know what's funny? I thought I might become a flight instructor."

"You'll be fine," he said. "You have your private license, don't you?"

"No. I've only got fourteen hours," I said.

"You've only got fourteen hours and you're out here flying in these crosswinds?" he asked.

"They weren't crosswinds when I took off," I said. He just laughed and shook his head. So I could add "crashing an airplane" to my list of dumbass accomplishments. The next time I went to do touch-and-go's there was a low cloud cover not much over the pattern altitude. My instructor was there that day. He missed my crash landing, but of course he had heard plenty about it.

That day when I was on final descent he came on the radio and said, "You better get your ass a little higher or you'll be plowing fields again."

As I continued flight training, I became a little more comfortable in the cockpit. I was still cautious on windy days. When it became time to do night training, we went to the Peoria airport. It had a control tower, and the runways were longer, wider, and better lighted. Flying at night does weird things to your senses. Without the visual references, your body sends you false signals. If you don't use your instruments, you can get into trouble fast. You can't really tell what attitude the plane is in. Pilots have flown into the ground thinking lights on the ground are stars, and they were going up. Even though my instructor was telling me I was doing well, my stress level was through the roof. Peggy came with me. She was sitting in the back seat enjoying the flight, and I was sweating and tense as hell. Part of the training was a simulation of loss of instruments and all lights. The instructor turned all the lights off and I had to fly and land using only runway lighting and the sound and feel of the plane. I managed not to kill us all, but it was definitely stressful. When I got out of the plane, I had an imprint of the control wheel in my hand because I had been gripping it so hard. It proved to be valuable training. In the near future it would help keep me alive.

I was almost finished with my training. The next part would be a cross-country flight, and then the written exam and a check ride with an FAA examiner. My cross country was going to be going from Mount Hawley to Moline, from there to Burlington, and then back to Mount Hawley. I had to file a flight plan. This involved calling flight service and checking the wind speed at different altitudes, and the weather along the route I would be flying. My instructor went with me the first time. The flight went as planned with no problems, and now I had to do it again alone.

The next week I had to cancel the flight twice, on account of weather conditions. The day I went I got a late start around 4 PM, but it wouldn't get dark until around 8 PM, so I thought I had plenty of time. According to flight service there was no significant weather at either destination. When I got close to Moline there were pretty dark clouds forming, and it started to rain. After I landed the rain and wind picked up, so I had to sit it out and see what happened. I was there for an hour or more before the rain let up, and I had to get going if I was going to get back before dark. I was in light rain all the way to Burlington. When I got there, I landed, had my logbook signed, and took off for home.

About halfway to Peoria the rain stopped, but it was getting dark. I just had my prescription sunglasses, not my regular glasses. It was really dark as I neared Peoria so I turned on all my lights. Nothing happened. Not a light on the plane came on. So I had no lights, my glasses were sunglasses, and I couldn't see shit for any distance. I was going to call the Peoria tower for traffic conditions. I could make out some moving lights but I couldn't tell their altitude. Guess what? The radio also didn't work. I guess the plane was getting me back for crashing it. I didn't know what else to do, so I went up to about five thousand feet when I went over the Peoria airport. I thought that would get me clear of any traffic arriving or leaving. I made it to Mount Hawley. Now all I had to do was land. The runway lights were on, but I couldn't see my instruments or any traffic. It took me two tries, but I managed to land without killing anyone. If I hadn't done the night training the week before, the story would have ended differently. It was around 8:45 PM when I entered the terminal. My instructor happened to be there. He said, "Are you just getting back?" I told him about the "no significant weather" I had encountered. He said he'd had similar experiences. What the flight service thought significant wasn't what he thought was significant. After telling him everything that had happened, he said I had done pretty well. I told him to make sure to tell the airport manager I didn't break the plane this time.

Even though I had enough hours, I never followed through with getting my license. I had pretty much given up the idea of being an instructor, and I really couldn't see any sense to getting the license. I could go up and fly without the license if I wanted to do so, but just flying around really isn't that exciting unless you crash land. To travel anywhere, the weather is always a factor. To be able to fly in any weather you need an instrument rating. In addition, you have to have a plane that has the equipment for all-weather flight. So basically, I was pretty much done with flying, and I knew I needed somewhere else to channel my interest. I knew I was not a changed person just because I hadn't been in any trouble lately. Both my mind and body needed a lot of work.

Finding the "Way" of Pain

Martial arts had always interested me. When I was in school at Purdue, they had a karate and judo club, but my class and study schedules never left me the time to join. I watched a few classes and it looked like something I would like to do. Other than that, my only exposure to martial arts was from television or movies. I had seen a karate school in Pekin, Illinois, which was about fifteen miles from Glasford. When I stopped flying, I went and signed up for karate. I'm sure you're thinking that this would not be a good thing for someone wanting to quit fighting. I admit that the same thought had crossed my mind. I can't truthfully tell you why I did it. I knew I needed to do something physical to get my mind and body in shape. As it turns out, for once in my life I made the correct decision, whatever the reason.

Karate do means "empty hand way." There are many styles of karate. The one I had joined was Shorei-Ryu, which was a style developed in Okinawa. Although I liked the art, the school's teaching methods left a lot to be desired. It was conducted in a very rigid military boot camp manner. They were very big into discipline, but not self-discipline. The teaching was done by the highest rank that happened to show up for class. In more than a year and a half of attendance, I was taught by a black belt only twice. Physically it got me into shape. Right after I joined the school, I also joined a Nautilus Health Center. I found that Nautilus machines took my body through the full range of motion, so I could improve both flexibility and strength.

Even though I didn't like the way the karate classes were run, I still went to class on a regular basis, and I practiced on my own between classes. I thought I was progressing reasonably well, so I decided I needed to go to a tournament to see how I stood up against students from another school The first tournament I entered in Indianapolis I got second place. The trophy was given to me by Bill "Superfoot" Wallace. At that time he was the PKA Middleweight World Champion, and he had played an assassin in one of Chuck Norris' movies. I had seen pictures of him giving a trophy to Elvis Presley. Since I never expected to win anything, and being the dumbass I am, I didn't have a camera! After the tournament, he gave an hour-long seminar. I was smart enough to attend that. He wasn't called "Superfoot" for nothing. His kicks had blinding speed, and he showed me what could be attained by training hard.

The pharmacist who had taken my job at Super-X in Bartonville was a Japanese-American. Since my karate class was taught in Japanese, I thought I'd ask him to help me with some of the Japanese terminology. The first time I met him he had big purple bruises on both his arms. It looked like someone had beaten him with a baseball bat. I asked him what happened, and he said "I was sparring with Master Kim." He was studying tae kwon do (a Korean martial art) under Master Soo Kon Kim in Peoria. Unfortunately he couldn't help with my problem. He didn't speak Japanese! He was born in an internment camp where his parents were held during World War II. He had trained in karate and judo before going to Master Kim.

I told him I wasn't happy with my training, and he told me to come and watch one of his classes. I went with him that night. Watching the class, I had mixed feelings about it. It was run completely differently than mine, and I was reluctant to change. I went to my class the next afternoon, and nobody showed up to teach it. That did it for me. That night I went and joined Master Kim's school. Besides marrying my wife, this was the best decision I ever made. It's because of that decision that I even have a life.

Karate is about sixty percent hand techniques and forty percent kicking. Most of the kicks are at waist level or below. Tae kwon do is a kicking art. It's about eighty percent kicking and twenty percent hand techniques. Tae kwon do is an ancient Korean art. Translated literally, tae means "to kick or smash with the feet." Kwon refers to "punching" or "destroying with the hand or fist." Do means "way" or "method." It is the "way" that is the heart of the art. A tae kwon do master can use punches, flying kicks, blocks, dodges, and interceptions with the hands, arms, and feet to bring about the rapid destruction of an opponent. With great power comes great responsibility. A developed tae kwon do technique gives power that should never be misused. Tae kwon do is a disciplining of the mind and body, but it is much more. The ultimate goal of studying and mastering tae kwon do is to find the way of serenity.

A master works for years to become a tranquil human being. He is calm and unafraid in disaster because he has become accustomed to the idea that every step draws him closer to death. His whole being is concentrated on achieving serenity and bringing others to that serene state with him. Master Kim is the embodiment of everything that is tae kwon do. He taught every class, and he was always there. He taught me more than kicking and punching. Every class he told us stories that pointed out the philosophies to be learned from martial arts. Everything he said made sense, and I began to understand that I could control my mind if I trained hard enough. He gave me a reason to stay alive. He started me on my journey to find the "way."

Because the kicks of tae kwon do are higher than those of karate, they were really difficult for my inflexible legs. Every time I tried to kick high with one leg, the other one left the floor also, and I crashed down to the floor. The floor was concrete under the rug, and repeated falls took a toll on my body. Trying to kick high also resulted in many pulled muscles. Since I never missed a class, they never had time to heal correctly. I stretched as much as I could, but I never seemed to accomplish anything but to inflame the tendons in my legs. Bill "Superfoot" Wallace advertised a "Power Stretcher" on ESPN and in Black Belt magazine. He could go past 180 degrees where his legs would be behind his body. Nothing else seemed to work, so I got a Power Stretcher.

They recommended that you only go until you had mild discomfort. I would go until I had mind numbing pain. I'd lock it there and watch TV while sitting that way. I'd stay that way for thirty minutes or so with the pain causing me to sweat buckets. When I released it, I had to pull my legs back together. The farthest I ever got was 135 degrees. I'm sure you're thinking "What a dumbass! Why put yourself in that much pain?" My body was in great pain, but my mind was becoming clearer. In all other aspects of my life, I could see everyday situations with a different perspective. The pain kept me focused. It made me develop a strong will. Drinking never entered my mind. The pain wouldn't let it.

There is a lot of pain involved in the martial arts. You cannot fight without pain. The first time you get hit with a good kick you think you're going to die. Then you realize that you're not dead, and if you concentrate, your mind can overcome the pain. I always had cracked bones in my hands, feet, and ribs. The ribs hurt the most. Every time you breathe it feels like getting hit again. Between the fighting and stretching, it was a toss-up which was causing me the most pain. I know it's hard for you to understand how this was helping me get my life back. The pain was always there reminding me to concentrate, and to control it in order to overcome it. It was not an easy thing to do, but I never missed a class or going to Nautilus to work out. As I progressed up the ranks toward my goal of black belt, my mind and my will became stronger.

Master Kim and the other serious students were always there with me, and the bond I formed with them has lasted a lifetime. I concentrated on the training, and it was soon time for my black belt test. Another student and my friend would be testing at the same time. He was younger and was really good, and of course I felt I was not ready. We both passed and became the second black belts Master Kim had promoted in the United States. I had discovered I could overcome pain and control my mind. Becoming a first degree black belt was only the beginning. I was only starting on the path to find my martial spirit.

Kicking a 180 pound water bag at my school.

Breaking boards for a demonstration in Peoria.

Sins of the Past

We moved into Peoria around the fourth year we'd owned the pharmacy. As far as most of the people in Glasford were concerned, I would never be anything but the crazy man who had tried to shoot the innocent children. Peggy and I still took turns working there, so I never had to spend too much time in the town. Every now and then I would go on a ride along with the town cop. Since he had become full-time, nothing much exciting happened there. I continued my study of tae kwon do and working out. Most of my friends were other martial art students. There were around eight or ten of us that had been with Master Kim from the beginning. We helped him build his school by doing demonstrations at local community functions, and every year or so the whole school would put on a demo in a local high school gym. The last one I did we filled the floor with students, and the crowd packed both sides of the gym.

Master Kim bought a bigger building on Main Street by Bradley University, and his school continued to thrive. We started having a yearly tournament at the Peoria YWCA. We'd have six rings going with more than a hundred competitors. So my time was spent trying to improve myself and helping others to do so. My friend Larry, the Bartonville cop, had gotten worse with his drinking, and it was starting to affect his family and job. He would talk to me about it, but he really wouldn't admit that he couldn't control it. One Sunday morning he called me and asked me to help him. It was around 8 AM, and he was coming off of a bad Saturday night. I asked him if he had started to drink yet. He said he hadn't, and I told him I would come and talk to him around noon.

After I hung up, I started thinking about it and decided that I had better not wait until noon. I jumped in the shower, dressed quickly, and went to his house. I got there around 9:30, and he had already had a couple of drinks.

"It's only been an hour or so since I talked to you. You told me you weren't going to drink. You couldn't last two hours?"

"I was only going to have a couple. I just needed something to stop the shakes."

"Sure you did. I wish I had a dollar for every time I told myself that. If I had waited until noon, you'd be real steady. The problem is that you're not stopping the shakes, you're only postponing them."

"I was only going to have a couple. You don't have to get mad at me just because you couldn't do it. I'm not as bad as you were."

"Then why to hell did you call me? You keep telling me you want to quit, but you don't listen to anything I say." I yanked him out of his chair and took him to the bathroom. "Look at that mirror. Is that you looking back? You're only forty-two. What about the guy you're looking at? You're a cop. If you were describing him as a suspect, would you say he was forty? Wake the fuck up. You look sixty! You're looking at a dead man."

"I don't know how to stop. How am I going to stop?"

"Do you have any sweat pants?"

"Yeah, I've got some. Why?"

"Go put them on. You want to know how to quit? I'm going to show you. Change your clothes. I'm tired of fucking around with you." While he was changing I poured out all the whiskey in the house I could find. He came back just as the last was going down the drain.

"What the hell are you doing?"

"You wanted my help. I'm helping. When we get back you won't able to drink it. You won't be able to get the bottle to your mouth. Today's either going to be the first or the last day of your life. Either way, you'll be better off." I took him to Nautilus. He was in really bad shape. I put him through a workout that almost killed him. He had to stop and puke twice. Amazingly it worked. For the next few weeks I went with him to make sure he worked out, but he started going on his own almost every day. The last time I saw him, he looked and sounded like his old self. As far as I know, he stayed sober until he died from cancer a few years later. His wife thanked me for turning him around. I told her that he did the hard part. I just got him started. In any case, I hope I paid him back for helping me. What goes around comes around.

So things were going pretty well for me. I had seen an ad in a pharmacy magazine that a small town south of Champaign wanted a pharmacy. I wanted out of Glasford, so I went to check it out. Sidney seemed like a nice little town. I talked to the doctor, the town bank president, and looked at a building next to the doctor's office that was for sale. It was a big building. I thought I could divide it in half and have the pharmacy in the front and a tae kwon do school in the back. I even found a new house in town that we could rent. I went back to Peoria thinking that maybe this would be a new start for me. Then the past came back to bite me on the ass.

I got a call one night from a Peoria detective. He said he wanted to ask me some questions. I knew I had done nothing wrong, so I told him to ask away. He wanted to know if I was married. Then he asked if I had ever been in a bar in the big shopping mall in Peoria. I had not been in that or any other bar for the past five years. He asked a few more questions, and then he asked if I would come and talk to him the next day. I agreed to do so and hung up. Peggy and her sister who was visiting us wanted to know what it was all about. I told them I really didn't know, but I had a bad feeling about it. It turned out to be worse than I imagined. I went to see the detective the next day, and he dropped the bomb on me.

"Thanks for coming in. We just need to get a few things straight. Are you sure that you weren't at that bar last week?"

"I haven't been in any bar any place in over five years."

"A girl was raped leaving that bar last week. A guy held her at gunpoint and forced her into the back seat of her car. She described him for the police artist. I think it looks like you." He slid the picture across the desk for me to see. You know how on TV the drawing always looks just like the guy? Well this drawing could have been either me or Michael Jackson. Other than being male, I could see no likeness at all.

"Come on. You seriously think this looks like me? If you do, I don't see how you made detective. How do you know me anyway?"

"She picked your picture out of a mug book. It was in one with gun-related crimes."

"Well you're both crazy. As for picking my picture out of a mug book, why was it in there? It was supposed to be taken out and the records sealed after my year's probation."

After some more questions, he asked me if I would stand in a lineup. I agreed to do it the next day. When I got home I called the lawyer I had before. He told me not to stand in the lineup. I should have listened to him, but I knew I had done nothing, and I couldn't believe I would be picked. So the next morning I went to the station for the lineup. I told them to have us say something, because my speech defect would definitely stand out. I forget exactly what we had to say. It was something like, "Get in the car." Can you guess who was the lucky winner? She said my hair was shorter, I was shorter, I wasn't as heavy, and I didn't sound like him. However, I was the man who raped her. So I was arrested, handcuffed, and taken to the jail for processing. I can't remember all of the charges; rape, sexual assault, assault with a firearm, and being a dumbass. On the way to the jail, I was kind of laughing to myself.

"What's so funny? Don't you understand that you're being arrested?"

"It's not 'funny' funny. I just find it hard to believe that after all the shit I've done in my life, and after all the work I've done to clean it up, I'm going to prison for something I didn't do. Kind of ironic, don't you think?"

"If you're innocent, you don't have anything to worry about."

"Yeah, that's what I thought too. Right up until you put the handcuffs on me".

He let me call Peggy to come and pick up my car. That was a really fun phone call. "Guess what, dear? I've been arrested for rape." When they were processing me, he asked me if I would take a lie detector test.

"Sure, right now. I might as well give you some more rope to hang me."

So before they locked me up, he and another detective took me to another building in town to take the test.

"Come on guys. Can't you take the handcuffs off before we walk through the middle of town? I'm not going to run, and if I do you can do me a favor and shoot me."

I think I was the one most surprised when I passed the test. The way things had been going for me, I figured this would be the last nail in my coffin. So they released me and apologized for any trouble they had caused me. I wasn't pissed at him. I knew he was just doing his job. The whole nightmare was a learning process for me. I'm not quite so quick to make a judgment when someone else is accused of something. I don't think I could ever be on a jury and not be influenced by my experience. I definitely made sure I got all of my records cleaned out. They caught the guy about a month later. His picture was in the paper when he was convicted. Not a person called me and said they saw my picture in the paper. I guess we didn't look so much alike after all. The experience did one other thing. It made me decide to leave Peoria.

Making the Move

You can't run away from yourself. However, changing locations can give you a chance to correct past mistakes. It was obvious that I was never going to be happy if I had to continue owning a pharmacy in Glasford. No matter what I did, I was never going to make up for past actions. I decided that it was time to move. Although Sidney was another small town, I could see some potential there. Because I wanted to move so badly, I made a couple of dumbass mistakes. There was a pharmacist who wanted to buy the store in Glasford. He had survived a bout with cancer, and he wanted a job that wouldn't be physically demanding. It would have been a good deal for him. Since I wanted to leave so badly, I made him a really good offer. At first he accepted, but then he started changing his mind every other day. It finally pissed me off so much I told him he wasn't smart enough to run a pharmacy. I really was trying to give it to him, and he was too dumb to take it.

I had already bought the building in Sidney. They had started building the pharmacy and the tae kwon do school. I had already rented a new house, and then this pharmacist starts with his dumb shit. So I made a dumbass decision. I closed the pharmacy but kept the store. The woman working there would run it for me. So although I had the pharmacy inventory, I had no cash to put into the new store. The bank in Sidney loaned me all the money I needed at interest over twenty percent. Of course the remodeling cost more than planned, and I paid more than I should have for the building. After buying additional inventory, I wound up deep in debt right from day one. I carried the entire pharmacy inventory around in my car for three days. If I had been stopped by the police for any reason, I would have had to come up with some really creative thinking to explain why I had a whole car filled with drugs.

Just like Glasford, Sidney was a small town without a cop. Guess where the local kids liked to hang out at night? The front steps of my building! They weren't as bad as the bunch in Glasford, and I didn't live on Main Street, but I still couldn't let them continue to gather there every night. If the cops had to respond to an alarm from the pharmacy, they would have no idea who was doing what if several people were around the front door. It could be a dangerous situation. Obviously I knew I could not repeat the Glasford incident. I'm a dumbass, but I'm not stupid. So I tried a different approach.

Before the store or the school opened, I had all the local tough guys come in and watch me work out on a heavy bag. I knew they didn't respect property or authority, but they would respect power. I told them they would have to find a different place to hang out at night, and explained why it had to be that way. I told them I didn't care what they did or where they did it. I didn't care about the rest of the town. I did however, care about my own property. Then I put my hand through a concrete block. I could tell from wide-eyed faces and whispering that I had made my point. My property was never touched. One of the kids became one of my tae kwon do students. He told me that when I first came to town, one of his friends told him he was going to wait six months until the pharmacy was fully stocked, and then break into it. After that day he'd changed his mind. It wasn't worth dying for. My mission was accomplished.

This kid came from a pretty bad family. Most of them were in trouble with the law on a regular basis, and never held a regular job for any length of time. I told him that he didn't have to be like them just because they were his family. I told him martial arts could do the same for him that it had done for me. I told him he would be judged by his actions, not his family background. There were people from different social levels in my class. There were even a couple of college professors. One of the professors baked this kid a birthday cake and brought it to class. This totally stunned him. I don't think he'd ever had a birthday cake in his life, and it was hard for him to believe that anyone, especially a college professor, cared enough to do that for him. Unfortunately his peer pressure had greater pull on him than the tae kwon do class, and he returned to his old ways. He got in trouble with the law a couple of times, and I let him come back to class both times. I understood what he was going through. I only saw him three times a week. His friends and family saw him every day. It was just like the way my sailor buddies had influenced me. I told him he would have to choose what life he wanted, and I would not let him come back if he got into trouble again.

He lasted a few months, and then he was involved in a car theft that landed him in the hospital in pretty bad shape. One of my students went to visit him, and he told her he wanted me to come to the hospital to visit him. I told her to tell him I would not go to him, but if he wanted to see me when he recovered, I would be happy to talk to him. She got mad at me, saying he could die, and I didn't care. I told her he made the decision that got him there, and he had to live or die because of it. He had options, and if he lived, he would again have options. If he chose to come to me for help, I would help him. It was up to him, not me, to choose his path. She remained mad at me, and I never saw him again until about ten years later.

I was working in a pharmacy in Champaign, and a woman was getting a prescription filled. She saw my name, and asked if I used to teach tae kwon do in Sidney. I told her yes, and she said I had probably saved her husband's life. She left without saying anything else. Her name didn't ring any bells for me. The next day her husband came in to see me. I didn't recognize him at first, but it was my old student. He told me he was ashamed to come to see me when he got out of the hospital, but I had made him decide to change his life. He got his GED to finish high school, and was now married with two kids. He had a good job in management of a local company. He told me I had changed his life. I told him I was very proud of him, but he was the one who changed his life. He had simply decided not to be a dumbass.

Doing Whatever it Takes

Sidney was a much better place to live than Glasford, but as far as business went, it was not far enough from a larger town. It was only twelve miles from Champaign-Urbana. Since they didn't have to drive far, most residents did their major shopping in the large chain stores there. I had borrowed so much for the remodeling that my monthly payment to the bank took most of the profit. Peggy had to work for other pharmacies to keep us afloat. I felt bad that she had to do it, but she never complained about it. Since I wasn't drinking and getting into trouble, we got along a lot better. She continued to be the anchor that kept everything together. When the town restaurant closed, I decided to take out most of the front of the store and put in a restaurant. The day we opened it we only had seating for twenty-four. We had four tables with four chairs, and eight stools at the counter. We had so many people standing in line I had to take out more of the drug items and add four more tables. We had a nice little restaurant. It opened at 6 AM and closed at 2 PM. It made enough profit to at least help pay the bills. I'll admit I liked having my own cook and soda fountain. When I was a kid I was only allowed to have one Coke a day. Now I could drink all I wanted!

The tae kwon do school was my main interest. I had two classes every night so the students could get in their three hours of class a week. Since I was older and not a world champion like Master Kim, I really didn't know if I would be a competent teacher. I found teaching to be even more demanding, boring, and frustrating than being a student. I had to be there every night, and when few or none of the students showed up, I would wonder why I wanted to be there. But I made sure I was there, and as time went on I had several dedicated students. To my surprise I found that I was not only teaching them, but learning from them as well. I never charged much for the class, and I never made anyone quit because they couldn't pay as long as they were serious about training. One student kept changing jobs, and I would teach him at all hours of the day and night to continue his training. He eventually made it to black belt. I used the money I made from the school to buy my toys; a big screen TV and a hot tub.

My classes were hard. I demanded a lot from my students, but I never asked them to do anything I couldn't or wouldn't do. I was serious about martial arts, and I tried to teach them that tae kwon do was more than learning to fight. I told them about my past mistakes and how martial arts had turned my life around. I told them only a fool learns from his own mistakes. A wise man learns from the mistakes of others. I told them the truth and tried to be a good example. It had been about five years since I had taken a drink of alcohol or been in a fight outside of class.

Even though I had classes every night, I still joined the Fitness Center in Champaign and worked out there three times a week. I'd get up at 6 AM and go work out on the machines. One of my students said he could do anything I could do. So I took him with me one morning. I did a light workout compared to my normal routine, and he did do everything I did. A couple of mornings later his grandfather came into the restaurant. He said, "What the hell did you do to my grandson? That boy can't even put on his clothes he's so sore. He hasn't been to work in two days." I told him what had happened and he laughed so hard he was crying. The student never challenged me again. His mother worked for me. I called her "Preacher" because she was always preaching at me. She couldn't see anything except the fighting in tae kwon do. Her son was one of my better students, but she pressured him into quitting. He's had some problems in his later life that he might not have if he had continued training. She now knows what I was trying to teach. She's sorry she didn't see it back then. She's the one who really talked me into writing this. I'm still trying to help him. I won't give up on him.

As the school progressed, my students wanted to start competing in tournaments. At that time martial arts were thriving, and there were many tournaments where many different styles competed. I tried to train my students to fight different styles, so they could have the ability and confidence to beat any style using their rules. I told them that there were no superior arts, only superior martial artists. There were very few times that we didn't bring home several trophies. These tournaments were not full contact, but you still had to fight hard. Of course I was proud of them when they won. What really impressed me more was how they handled losing. I kept telling them that sometimes you learn more from losing than wining. That was the attitude they adopted. If they lost, instead of being depressed and moping around, they learned why they lost and trained even harder. Evidently I was getting through to them.

Around this same time period, full contact professional fights began. There were two different organizations, the Professional Karate Association, and the World Karate Association. Many of the fights were carried on ESPN. Chuck Norris and Bill "Superfoot" Wallace were two of many fighters who became well known in the martial arts world. I knew some fighters in Peoria who fought in the PKA, so we went there to train with them, and decided that we wanted to move up to full contact fighting. We built a ring in our school, and soon we had several people coming to train with us. I still laugh when I think about the first night of sparring. Everyone's adrenaline levels were off the chart, and everyone fought as hard as they could. Most everyone was bleeding before the night was over. The school was in the back half of the building. It was a hundred by fifty foot building I had divided in half with the pharmacy and restaurant in the front half. The bathroom was in the back half in the school. When I went to the restaurant the next morning, my cook said, "What the hell went on back there last night? It looks like someone was slaughtering hogs in the bathroom." I told her we were just having fun beating the hell out of each other. She just shook her head and told me to clean the bathroom.

Full contact fighting is vastly different from regular martial arts training. It combines the best hand techniques with the best kicking techniques, which are western boxing and Korean kicking. That's the way I train all of my students. I teach them the traditional forms and philosophies, but our fighting style is essentially the same as used in the ring. If you're not in martial arts, it's difficult to understand the difference. It's hard for some martial artists to understand.

I had several students from other schools find this out the hard way. A second degree black belt who taught karate at Parkland College came and wanted to fight. I put him in with Jim, my best fighter, and I instructed Jim not to hit him with anything. I just wanted to see how he moved with him. In three rounds, he never hit Jim with anything substantial either punching or kicking. The next time he came, I gave him a chest protector to put on. He said, "I'm a black belt. I don't need that." I made him wear it, and told Jim he could go to the body, but no head contact. I videotaped those three rounds. It was brutal. Jim hit him with so many body kicks all you could hear on the tape were the thuds of the kicks and his groans of pain. He never scored any points in any of the rounds. I told him if he came back, the head gear was going on and it would be real contact fighting. He never came back. He was a good sport about it. Jim is a painter. He was painting at the college a month or so later, and a karate class was going on. The instructor stopped class and introduced him, and told his class that he had been taught a valuable lesson by him in the full contact ring.

Jim was my first black belt. The week before his test, I decided to give him a pre-test to see if he was as good as I thought he was. On a hot July Sunday afternoon, I had him work out with me. It was close to one hundred degrees in the school. We had a hard-core workout, doing everything hard with no water or breaks. It was long. I guess it was probably around three hours. I was trying to make him quit. We ended with sit-ups, with our legs up on a weight bench. I meant to do five hundred. Then I thought we'd just keep going.

At seven hundred he asked, "Can I get a drink?" I said yes, but then we'd have to start again. He said, "Never mind." At one thousand we stopped. He never quit on me, and I knew I'd trained a real martial artist. He said he'd never sweat so much in his life. He easily passed his test the next weekend. Master Kim and other black belt friends of mine came from Peoria for his test. After the test we had a steak dinner in my restaurant for my students and their families. I don't know about him, but for me it was one of the few highlights of my life. It was great to hear Master Kim and the other black belts comment on how impressed they were with my students. More importantly, seeing all of them together with their families, seeing the bonds they were forming, made me feel that maybe I was making a positive difference in their lives.

Although the school was keeping me going mentally and physically, the town was fading away, and the pharmacy and restaurant were going with it. The pharmacy was killed by the same thing that killed all independent pharmacies and some chains—insurance companies. It only took one to kill my business. About two-thirds of the local doctor's patients joined it, so I had no choice but to accept it. The only other pharmacy that accepted it was Jerry's IGA in Urbana, and the guy that owned that pharmacy also owned the company that controlled the payment of the claims. Basically they paid me what and when they wanted. If I billed them fifteen hundred dollars, they might send me eight hundred or nine hundred dollars in a month or so. He was in St. Louis where the company was located. I had to threaten to get on a plane and come and take it out of his ass to get paid. He'd say if I didn't like it, I didn't have to accept it. He had me either way. If I quit, they had to go to his pharmacy. If I didn't, I had to live with his payments. I asked a lawyer about it. He said it wasn't illegal. It was definitely unethical, but not illegal. He also said I probably shouldn't go beat the bastard to death. So the pharmacy was basically in the toilet. The restaurant died with the town. They closed the train station. A couple of other businesses were defeated by Farm & Fleet and large department appliance stores. A bus tour business moved away. A world renowned artist moved his studio into Champaign. All in all, about twenty people who ate in the restaurant every day were gone.

Before all of this happened, I added another dumbass move that actually turned out to be okay. I bought a movie theater in Villa Grove. The bank was going to close it, so I went to look at it. It was a nice theater, and it had a three-room apartment above it. I asked the bank if I needed any money to buy it. They said no, so I took it. One of the women who worked in my restaurant needed a place to live, so I let her live there if she'd run the theater. It was kind of nice. I always wanted a movie theater, and I never had to do anything but go to the movie free every weekend. It actually made us a little money. A guy who owned a pizza place in Villa Grove got me started making pizza in my restaurant.

So I had a pharmacy, a restaurant, a pizza place, a martial arts school, and a movie theater. When you find yourself in a hole, keep digging dumbass. A week or so after I bought the movie theater I got a letter from the insurance company saying they wouldn't insure the theater because it showed porn movies. This was news to me! I went to the insurance company and asked them how they had come up with this revelation. They showed me a picture of the marquee that read *Once Upon a Mattress*. After laughing my ass off I asked the guy if he'd ever actually seen a porn movie. *Once Upon a Mattress* was a play the local theater group was performing about "The Princess and the Pea." It was nice to know I wasn't the only dumbass in the world. When we opened the theater we had a free showing of *The Karate Kid*. We did a demonstration on the stage before the movie. I think I made more of an impression than the kid in the movie. I got invited back to Villa Grove several more times to do demonstrations.

As fun as all of this was, it was time to end all of this madness. Another funny thing happened in Sidney before I started thinking about how to close everything out. The bank got audited. When they found out that the bank president had loaned me seventy thousand dollars on my signature alone (five thousand dollars for the down payment on the building that *his wife owned*), they gave him three months to get the money or collateral for the loan. He came to the store and told me this, and I never said a word. After a few minutes he left. I thought a minute, and then went to the bank. I threw the store keys on his desk and sat down and stared at him. He looked at the keys, then looked at me, then the keys. I just sat there.

"What's going on? What are you doing?"

"Maybe I didn't understand you. Did you or did you not just come and tell me that in three months you're going to call in my loan? A loan that I've never missed a payment on, at an interest rate that was so outrageous you just couldn't pass it up. I figure it's roughly thirty thousand dollars. Sound about right? Well I don't have thirty thousand dollars today, and I'm not going to have it in three months. So guess what? I'm not going to work for you for nothing for three months. Here are all your keys. If I were you, I'd go lock the door before they carry off the inventory."

I looked at my watch. "Me? I'm going to go to work out. Oh, by the way, I really would like to hear you explain how your wife happens to be the owner of the building." I got up and starting walking out of the bank. He was following right behind me.

"Wait a minute! Wait a minute! You can't do this!"

"I've sent the employees home. It looks to me like there are some customers in there. You probably should go protect your store." He was as pale as a ghost. I thought he might have a stroke any minute.

"I'll probably be home tomorrow if you come up with a plan. Don't call too early, though. I'll probably sleep in." Then I went to the Fitness Center to work out. Sometimes being a dumbass is really fun.

The next day I went to talk to him and we worked out a plan. His wife agreed to take back the building on a quit claim deed. That would take care of the building loan, and I would start closing the restaurant, pharmacy, and tae kwon do school. I would sell all of the equipment to pay on the loan. Although the restaurant was making a profit, it was also the only area that had payroll expenses, so it was the first to go. Selling the restaurant equipment was pretty easy. The tae kwon do school had nothing of value to sell, so all I had to do was stop the classes. I sold the movie theater for basically what I owed on it, so that was pretty much a break-even deal. That just left the pharmacy. Osco in Urbana agreed to buy my inventory if they got the prescription files. The only stipulation was that I had to agree not to work for any other pharmacy in Urbana for the next three years. I got a loan at a bank in Urbana and paid off the amount that I still owed to the Sidney Bank. Since I had never missed a loan payment, the new bank loaned me the money on just my signature. It only took a year or so to pay them off.

I had taken a job at the Veterans Hospital in Danville. I was not looking forward to working there. I had never worked in hospital pharmacy. It was going to be a forty-five minute drive, and I would be working for the federal government again. The only good part was my time in the Navy would count toward seniority, so I started the job at a higher pay grade and better benefits. Of course it was as screwed up as the military. First they said I had only been in the Navy six years, since I only had the discharge papers for the last six years. It was an uphill battle for quite a while, but finally they found the discharge papers from the first year. I even showed them my graduation book from boot camp, which clearly showed I was definitely there when I said I was, but they never gave in until they found the discharge.

Then they came up with another brilliant request. They said I would have to give them a certain percent of all the money I had made in my seven years of service in the Navy, and that would be put into my retirement fund. I said, "So I'm going to wind up paying taxes on the same money three times."

"That's not true," they said.

I tried to get them to explain why it wasn't true.

"I paid taxes on the money when I made it in the Navy. Is that right?" I asked. They agreed. Then I said, "I paid taxes on the money I'm going to give you now. Is that right?" They agreed. I then said, "When you give me this money back, I'm going to have to pay taxes on it again. Is that correct?" Again they agreed. So I said, "That's the third time I'll be paying taxes on the same money. Isn't that right?"

"No, it's not,"

"Please explain why it's not,"

"It's just not," they said.

It was typical government logic. Luckily I had only made twenty-two thousand five hundred dollars in seven years in the Navy. I can't wait until they give it back to me so I can pay the taxes again!

Free Falling—Learning to Fly

Acouple of years before I closed the tae kwon do school, I mentioned in class one night that I had once signed up for a skydiving class. It turned out that the Saturday I was supposed to go to the class was the day I was scheduled to take my black belt test, so I never got to take the class. One of my students asked if I still was interested. He was a skydiver, and they had classes every weekend. All I had to do was go to the Danville airport at 9 AM on Saturday or Sunday to take the class. So the next Sunday morning I went to the class, and so began another great passion of my life. The class started at 9 AM and there were sixteen other people in the class.

The guy teaching the class was a good instructor. He reminded me of the instructors I had when I was in Nuclear Prototype School. I found out later there was a good reason for that. He had actually been an instructor at the same prototype where I had qualified, and he went from there to duty on the USS Tullibee (SSN-597). As if that wasn't amazing enough, one of the regular skydivers worked at the same site in Windsor Locks as a civilian contractor. What are the odds of the three of us meeting in central Illinois? The instructor was as thorough here as he had been at the prototype. He went through the parts of a parachute, how they operated, and all of the emergency procedures in case something went wrong. This took about three hours, and then we had an hour break for lunch. When I went outside the plane was on jump run, so I would get to see some actual skydivers in action. The first two people out of the plane had malfunctions and had to use their reserves. One of them was the student who had brought me to the class. The other was the ex-wife of the instructor. They both landed under their reserves with no injuries. Remarkably, seeing two malfunctions in a row never bothered me. I never gave it a second thought.

After lunch we had a written test, and then went over the test to make sure we understood any of the questions we had gotten wrong. Then we had harness training. They hung us up in a parachute harness and went through all the potential problems and how we should handle them. After completing this, it was time to jump. The plane could only take a jump master and three students at one time. I was going to be in the third load. The parachute and equipment were the same the military used. The parachute was a round T-10 and we would be using a static line that would open the chute. We wore coveralls, combat boots, helmet, goggles, and a "belly wart" reserve parachute. The instructor tightened the harness so tight I could hardly breathe. So basically, I was hotter than hell, could hardly breathe or walk with all the gear on, and scared shitless.

The plane was a Cessna 182. After we were all loaded, it was pretty jammed up. Last in would be the first out. I was going to be first. We took off for the jump altitude of three thousand feet. At one thousand feet, the jump master hooked up the static line of the first student. On the climb to altitude I was sweating my ass off and my mouth was so dry my tongue was sticking to the roof of my mouth. The jump master whose name was "Crazy Larry," was talking all the time telling me it would be fun, to relax, and to follow his instructions. Then we were on jump run at three thousand feet.

When Crazy Larry unlatched the door, it flew up under the wing with a bang and stayed there. We were flying along with Larry hanging out the door looking for the drop point. My mind was on an adrenaline overload. Then it was time. Larry yelled, "Cut," and the pilot cut the

154

engine and slowed to about eighty miles per hour. Then Larry said, "Sit in the door," and I swung my feet out the door onto a step that's over the wheel. The wind was much stronger than I expected. He yelled, "Climb out," and I tried to get out on the step while working my way hand over hand up the wing strut until I'm hanging on the strut with my feet off the step. As I was climbing out, it occurred to me that I was trying not to fall.

I thought, "Why the hell am I trying not to fall? I'm going to jump anyway." I was supposed to look at him at this point and let go when he gave the signal. However, I did not look at him, but I was fixated on the wing.

I heard him yell "Go." Again I heard "Go," and I was still there.

I thought, "Let go, dumbass. He said 'go.' Why am I still hanging on?"

Finally, on the third "Go," I let go. There was a strong jerk, then it was quiet and I was floating toward the ground. Damn! What a rush! Believe me you'll never forget your first jump.

Under a round T-10 parachute you're pretty much at the mercy of the wind. It only has a five miles per hour forward speed. As far as the landing goes, it's about like jumping off a six-foot step ladder. To avoid injury you must do a parachute landing fall, which entails keeping your feet together and immediately rolling on your side on the ground. It's not a gentle landing, which is why you wear combat boots. I landed on the airport, but got dragged about twenty-five feet before I could get up and collapse the chute. This is another bad characteristic of round parachutes. As I was walking back, hotter than hell with all the gear on and the chute wrapped around me, my mind was still trying to process exactly what had happened.

Peggy walked out to meet me and asked how it was. The first thing I said was, "I'm never going to do this again!" It took quite a while for the adrenaline rush to end, and then I was really tired. The funny part is that I really couldn't remember the whole experience. It's called "hysterical amnesia." Your mind is totally overwhelmed by the adrenaline overload. One jump is usually enough for most people. Like martial arts, only about three out of one hundred continue. Of course by now you know enough about me to guess what I did. The next weekend I did my second and third jumps. You have to make five static line jumps before you start to free fall. Believe it or not, the next weekend Peggy went to the class and made her first jump. We were on the same load when I was making my fifth and she was on her third. She quit after that, and I really couldn't blame her. It was physically demanding on me, so I know it was really hard for her. I'm proud of her for doing three jumps. She's done something that a large percent of the population including so-called tough guys are afraid to do.

On the last three static line jumps they put a "dummy ripcord" on you. You have to pull it and show it to the jump master before you're cleared for free fall. I was ready! The first free fall is called a hop-and-pop. You let go of the plane and immediately pull your ripcord. Sounds simple, doesn't it? Of course, nothing is as simple as it sounds. You can't look down at your ripcord. Your body follows your head. Look down and you're upside down immediately. Can you guess what this dumbass did? You got it. I let go and looked at the ripcord as I was pulling it. I was upside down immediately with the parachute going out between my legs. It started to wrap around my right leg and I kicked as hard as I could. It came off my leg and opened while I was head down. The opening shock jerked me right side up so hard it almost knocked me out. I managed to complete the jump, but I was definitely in a low state of mind. When the plane landed, Crazy Larry got out and looked at me. He just shook his head and walked away. They say you never forget your first jump, first free fall, or first malfunction. I knew then that they were right about the first two. Anyone but a dumbass would be happy knowing two out of three.

When I went back the next weekend, I took Jim with me. While we were sitting around waiting for me to make my second free fall, he said, "I've never seen you apprehensive about anything." I always told my students it was okay to feel fear, but you can't let fear control your actions.

I told him, "Last week I almost killed myself, and it's really hard for me to make myself get back in that plane. If I don't do it again, fear wins. I can't teach you that you can control fear, and then not be able to do it myself. All week I've been doing what I tell you to do. I've been training to control my body to overcome the fear." I made a dummy ripcord and practiced until I knew I could make my body perform correctly even if my mind still felt the fear. I made the jump correctly, and started progressing through the free fall training. The next step was two jumps at five seconds before pulling, then two at ten, fifteen, and twenty seconds. You start hitting terminal velocity (around 120 miles per hour) at around ten seconds. This is when the downward force of gravity equals the upward force of drag, and it's when you really start learning to fly. All you have to do is fall belly to earth in a stable position. It sounds so simple. It was the most frustrating time of my life. It was even worse than learning martial arts. My dumbass side said quit, but I never listened to it. My training kicked in. I was going to control my mind and make myself continue. It was proof to me that I was making progress.

Although it was exciting, I really wasn't having that much fun. It seemed the harder I tried the worse I did. It was not until my twelfth or thirteenth jump that I finally got relatively stable and was falling belly to earth. The parachutes we were jumping were still round, but had more control than the T-10 with the static line. Even though they were bigger, the landing was still hard and the wind pretty much controlled where you landed. As I was walking back to the drop zone with the chute wrapped around me, sweating my ass off, I kept thinking that maybe this sport wasn't for me. I decided to give myself twenty-five jumps to make up my mind. If it didn't start being more fun, I was going to give it up.

As usual, things didn't go quite like I planned. On my fifteenth jump, I had my first and only malfunction—a line caught over the middle of the chute—and had to cut the chute away. By the way, they're right when they say you never forget your first jump, first free fall, or first malfunction. It was definitely an adrenaline rush. The "belly wart" reserve might be uncomfortable, but you tend to overlook that after it saves your life. Again my training came into play. I never hesitated a second to get rid of the malfunction. My body was reacting the way my mind was telling it. In skydiving, it's extremely important to react quickly and correctly. Sometimes hesitating as little as five seconds may cost you or someone else their life.

On my next jump I was given a canopy that I'd never jumped before. It was an old Para-Commander that was modified for competition. I was told it would come down faster than the others I had jumped. My free fall and opening were pretty good, but as I was coming down I was headed for a bulldozer that was working on a runway.

I thought, "They said this chute had a faster forward speed, so I'll turn around and run past the bulldozer, then turn back into the wind to land." So I turned to run with the wind, and the ground came up and smacked the shit out of me. I don't know how fast I was going when I hit, but it felt like a truck had hit me. I bounced and rolled several times right beside the bulldozer, and stopped on my stomach with my face in the dirt. It knocked the wind out of me, and I knew something on my right leg was broken. I lay there until my breath came back, but I was afraid to move. After a few minutes nobody came to get me, so I slowly started to move a little at a time. I was thinking, "Maybe I only sprained my ankle." I got up, and immediately went back down.

Finally they came and got me. My right foot was swollen to about three times its normal size, but other than that I seemed to have nothing else broken. They carried me to my car, and I drove myself home. I called the town doctor to meet me at his office to check me out. He had to cut my shoe off. My foot was twice the size of a football and many ugly colors. The x-ray showed my right heel bone was totally shattered. He wanted to hospitalize me and put pins in it to put it back together. I said no to that. I didn't have any insurance, and I couldn't be away from the store that long. He then said we'd wait until the swelling went down and then put a cast on it. I said no to that also. I said "It'll heal."

The next day I got a chair with rollers, put my knee on it, and worked that way. The pain was unbelievable. Jim taught the class, and I worked every day and got into the hot tub every night. I was on crutches for six months. The first day on the crutches was the only time I felt unable to defend myself, but it didn't take long for me to figure out how to use the crutches as weapons if necessary. The last time my foot was x-rayed, the doctor said that if I'd let him do the surgery, it would probably have looked better but probably wouldn't have the mobility. He agreed that as long as I was going to continue skydiving and martial arts, it was probably going to be broken again anyway. It continued to hurt for years. I found out that every member of the Illiana Skydivers who had broken anything had done it jumping that same chute. They finally stopped using it and made a car cover out of it. I wish some dumbass had thought of that before I jumped it.

Skydivers are a lot like sailors. They love to party! For the first five years I never partied with them, but since I no longer practiced martial arts on a regular basis, I lost my discipline. The World Free Fall Convention is one long party. The guys from my drop zone never tempted me that much. At the convention there were five thousand of them to influence me. Basically they jump all day and party all night. Still, I never came close to returning to the person I'd been before. All the training I have done will never let me lose control as I once did. The dark side is still there, but now it's only a light grey. My mind is aware that the demons are always going to be waiting in the shadows. I can't remember ever coming close to fighting. I did, however, drive and jump when I was a long way from being completely sober. I was just lucky. Sometimes your luck runs out. I've had four friends killed jumping, and others busted up pretty badly. Only one friend was killed who was on the same jump with me. Like I've said, it's a dangerous and unforgiving sport.

Top Gun

Being a fighter pilot is the only job I consider worth having. It takes an aggressive personality to become a fighter pilot. They each really believe that they're the best pilot flying. If you get one hundred fighter pilots in a room and tell them that they're going on a mission that ninety-nine won't be returning from, each pilot will look around the room and think, "Those poor guys are soon going to be dead." When I teach martial arts students, I try to instill that kind of thinking in their training. I try to give them the mind of a tiger. I want them to really believe that they can defeat anyone or anything that confronts them in their life. Even if it seems impossible to succeed, they will never stop trying. When I was applying to flight school, I had that cocky attitude. Looking back, I realize that my mind probably wasn't strong enough to back it up. It's ironic that when my body was young and strong, my mind didn't have the discipline necessary to back it up. Now that my mind is strong from years of training, my body is not capable of doing the job.

It should come as no surprise that my favorite movie is *Top Gun*. In fact, Tom Cruise stars in both of my favorite movies: *Top Gun* and *The Last Samurai*. The military's Top Gun schools give today's fighter pilots the chance to find out if they are really the best of the best. They learn to apply the art of dogfighting in today's world of high performance fighter planes. They find out that the tactics have not changed since the first time dogfighting began. Everything else being equal, it's still the pilot that makes the difference. The high speeds, and strong G forces make a pilot push his plane and body to the absolute edge of endurance. Being second best means you're dead. The incentive to be the winner could be no higher.

I'll never know if I would have made it as a fighter pilot. I do know that I tried my best to get a chance to find out. However, I did get a chance to find out what it was like to be in a dogfight. There's a place in Houston, Texas called the Texas Air Aces. The instructors there are all ex-fighter pilots. They fly T-34 fighter trainers with radar guns in the wings. When you fire the guns you hear the machine gun sound in your earphones, and if you score a hit the other plane begins to trail smoke. Since you have an instructor in the back seat, anyone can get the experience. They let you fly as much as you're able. Even pilots who are current fighter pilots go there to hone their dogfighting skills. It's as close as I would ever get to fly a fighter plane, so I signed up for the course.

Since I can fly an airplane, I signed up for two days. The day before I was going to do the dogfighting, I wanted to do aerobatics in the plane to get a feel of how the plane flew. I also got a computer game that simulated flying World War II planes and practiced doing aerobatic maneuvers that way. When I got there it was raining and had been for days. Again I had outsmarted the dumbass side of me. I had taken ten days vacation hoping that there would be a couple of days of good weather during that time. It turned out that was a smart decision. It finally stopped raining.

The instructor I had for the aerobatics was an ex-Navy pilot. He had lived the life I had envisioned for myself. He flew F-4 Phantoms in Vietnam, and then moved up to F-14 Tomcats later in his career. He did two tours of duty at Top Gun school. All of the instructors had flown in combat. They were definitely cool guys. They had a sign hanging up that read: There are only two types of airplanes. Fighters and targets! We went up with another plane that was going to do some other type of exercise. I got to practice formation flying with the other plane. It's not as simple as it looks. Then the other plane took off and we went to do the aerobatics. My instructor asked if I had ever done aerobatics. I told him I had done advanced aerobatics in a glider, but I didn't do the piloting. It was just a fun ride. I told him I had read the instruction manuals they had sent me, and practiced them on the computer planes. So when we got to the airspace we were assigned, he gave me control of the plane and said he'd tell me what to do and talk me through.

For forty minutes or so we were continually doing different maneuvers. G force, or the force of gravity, goes from positive to negative throughout the maneuvers. We were constantly going from positive four G's to negative four G's. It was as if I had seven hundred pounds sitting on me pushing me into the seat one minute, and then I'd be floating in the harness the next. Modern fighter pilots wear G-suits. This suit keeps the blood from pooling in the legs and the pilot from passing out. Six G's can cause you to pass out, and modern fighter planes can turn at nine G's or higher. By the time we were done I was completely worn out. The constant G forces I experienced were tough on my body. As we were taxiing in, I told him my favorite movie was *Top Gun*. He said he had done the flying for "Viper" in the movie. I had gotten to fly with one of my movie heroes!

The next day for the dogfighting my instructor was ex-Air Force. During the first Gulf War he was put in charge of an A-10 Thunderbolt squadron. He said he was mad at first. The A-10 was not a fighter plane. He said that his attitude changed the first time he fired the cannon. From that time on he loved that airplane. The dogfighting really wasn't as fun as doing the aerobatics. We were limited to a certain space of sky, so basically it was just a turning fight. The planes would meet head on quite a bit apart, and when we were equal they would call "fight's on."

My adrenaline was really pumping and in the first encounter I snatched it up into a six G turn. I almost passed out, and the instructor commented that I didn't have to be quite so aggressive. The guy I was fighting wasn't a pilot, but it really didn't matter. I knew that I was fighting his instructor. We took turns being the target or the attacker. The instructors made sure everyone got to win an equal amount. I fouled up the last time, though. I was the target. I pulled another six G tight turn, stalled the plane, and went inverted before I recovered. It definitely threw off their attack! After we landed, the other instructor asked if I had done it on purpose. I confessed that I had lost the plane in the turn. He said it definitely kept me from getting shot down. If it had been a real dogfight, I would still be alive!

It was a fun experience, but it was still not the same as flying a real military fighter plane. I didn't think I'd ever get to experience that. It's almost impossible unless you're very rich or some well-known celebrity. Little did I know that a few years later I'd get to fly a Russian MIG! This was an actual military jet fighter plane. It cost me two thousand dollars, but it was worth every penny. I got to fly for about twenty minutes and did some combat six G maneuvers. Then the owner took over and did some really cool flying. I was very tired and very happy when we landed. It was an experience I'll never forget.

My heroes are the Blue Angels. I would do or pay anything to fly with them. I'm pretty sure that it'll never happen, but I've learned that if you stop being a dumbass, the impossible might become possible. Who knows, if enough people buy this book, maybe I'll be famous enough to rate a ride! A slim chance is better than no chance at all.

Top gun
for an hour.

Flying a Russian MIG.
A chance of a lifetime!

Getting Higher/Going Faster

Skydiving is more addictive than drugs. It has a lot in common with martial arts. No matter how good you get, you always want to be better. Both activities require total concentration. If you lose your concentration when you're fighting, you can either hurt your opponent or yourself. Losing your concentration in free fall can cause you to die quickly, and it puts the other jumpers in the air with you in danger also. Hitting someone too hard with a punch or kick can result in bruises or broken bones. Hitting someone in free fall at over 120 miles per hour usually results in death or very serious injuries. So skydiving is the most unforgiving sport. Sometimes your first mistake is also your last, and you can die on your first or your ten thousandth jump. So why do I do it? I do it because it is so demanding. Both martial arts and skydiving make me strive to control my mind and body. Neither sport is for everyone. Both require total commitment to excel in them. Even though they wreak havoc on my body, they make me work harder to control my mind. I've been doing both for many years, and I still have a lot to learn.

Most people think skydivers have a death wish. In the twenty-four years that I've been doing it, I can't think of anyone with that attitude. Since I've experienced that feeling several times for many years, I can usually spot it in others. The skydivers come from all walks of life. They all know it's a dangerous sport, but if done correctly, you're in more danger driving to the airport than jumping out of an airplane. I think I would say we're all adrenaline junkies. I can't think of anything that comes close to the high-speed excitement unless it's driving a race car at two hundred miles per hour in a bumper-to-bumper race. Flying a high performance airplane and doing aerobatics at high G-forces also comes close. So I don't think it's a death wish. It's pushing your mind and body to the limit and controlling the outcome. I admit that I've been suicidal for several years, and there have been times that I'd go to the airport and not get into the plane because of my frame of mind. I never exit the aircraft worried that I will be hurt or killed. My main concern is not to do anything that puts another jumper in danger. So it's just the way I am. When someone can't see why anyone would jump out of an airplane, when the door opens and there's the beautiful blue sky and white clouds, I can't imagine why they wouldn't want to.

Going to the convention became a tradition for me. I never missed one for ten years. One year I got to try a new kind of jumping, called bungee jumping. Most people say they wouldn't sky dive because they're afraid of heights. The truth is that you don't have a height sensation if you're not attached to the ground. I've got a friend with twenty-five hundred jumps but won't get up on a step ladder. You don't even get a falling sensation because the airplane is moving. Bungee jumping is totally different. You are attached to the ground. In this case it was a tall crane, and I definitely got a falling sensation and ground rush. So when about ten of us went to do the bungee jump, none of them would go unless I went first.

I admit I was hesitant to do it. I don't really like high places either. Because I felt some fear, it was really important for me to do it. Overcoming the fear would reinforce my confidence that I could make my mind control my body. I couldn't chicken out in front of all of them, so I was the first to go up. It was definitely a rush! Diving headfirst toward the ground really gets your adrenaline up. I'm glad I did it, but unlike skydiving, it took no skill to do, only the courage to jump. I didn't see the point of paying sixty dollars to jump from one hundred feet, when I could jump from fifteen thousand feet for twenty dollars. So once was enough for me. It was one more experience to add to my life. I'll admit that I'm driven to prove to myself that I can do anything I want to do. They can put on my tombstone, "Now I've done everything!"

I stopped jumping about five years ago and sold my parachute, but now I've bought a new one and started jumping again. This year I was going to jump two new things: a glider and a balloon. I was geared up waiting on the glider, and when he landed he crashed into the back of a pick-up truck. So there went the glider jump. The next morning I got up at 4:15 AM to jump from a balloon. When they were filling it, there was a very large hole in it. So there went the balloon jump. There's always next year.

You definitely go fast in free fall. You can go from 120 miles per hour to more than 200 miles per hour, depending on your body position. You don't really get the speed sensation unless you pass someone going slower or someone deploys his parachute next to you. So a speed junkie like me still needs another way to get the speed fix. Fast cars are a natural choice. Corvettes have always been my favorite car, and ever since my first one in 1975, I have always had a Corvette. They just keep making them better and faster. I've had a '75, '84, '92, '98 Indy 500 Pace Car convertible, '02, '03 50th Anniversary Edition, '04 Le Mans Edition convertible, and a 400 HP '05. I generally drove them somewhere every weekend to go skydiving. When a lot of the drop zones closed and I stopped skydiving, I really didn't drive them enough to justify what they were costing me, so I sold the '05. This was the first time in thirty years that I didn't have a Corvette. The flying, skydiving, bungee jumping, and fast cars were a way for me to channel my driving forces to things other than drinking and fighting.

When I did have the Corvettes, I wanted to go to a driving school to learn to drive them better. There is a driving school in Las Vegas that uses Corvettes for their school cars. I wanted to go there, but for one reason or another I never made it. Peggy saw an ad for Richard Petty's NASCAR driving school and asked me if I wanted to go to it. I really hadn't thought about driving a NASCAR, but a six hundred horse power would definitely go fast, so I told her to try to find one I could attend. The only one that fit our schedule was in Milwaukee at the Milwaukee Mile Speedway. It was a one-day school, and only cost $350 to do eight laps on the track. So I signed up and we went on a three day weekend. Of course my bad luck followed me, and the day I was scheduled it rained all morning. When it stopped raining, they used machines to dry the track. There were ten of us in the class, and we picked numbers to determine when we went. Guess who picked number ten. Of course it was me. They took us around the track in a van and explained how we were supposed to drive the course. We would follow one of the instructors in a car in front of us, and if we were doing okay, we would increase speed on every lap. If you had any problems, they would stop you and talk about it before they let you continue.

Going last was both good and bad. I got to watch the others and see their mistakes. A couple of them got stopped a couple of times, but it gave me more time to get nervous, and the sky looked like more rain was coming. The sky was nothing but dark clouds when my time finally came. The first problem was getting into the car. The doors don't open, so you have to climb in through the window. I made it into the car, and my adrenaline was pumping when we took off. Evidently I was doing okay because we kept going faster every lap. The cars had no speed odometers, so I don't know how fast I actually went. Our laps were timed, and they gave us a printout of our lap average. Mine was 119.8 miles per hour, so I was probably only going around 150 miles per hour on the straightaway. I know I wanted the guy to get out of my way. As soon as my turn was over, I did a ride around with one of the instructors "racing" another instructor. He almost lost it in one of the corners, and said he was sorry about it. I thought it was great!

Author with NASCAR at Milwaukee Mile Speedway.

I've been jumping out of this same plane for twenty-four years.

Missing man formation for a jumper who died on the jump a week before.
(Author left of open space.)

Bungee jump at a skydive convention. Major ground rush!

PRESENT DAY

The process of writing down my life experiences has changed the way I think about them. That's the way life happens. All your plans and expectations can change at any time. Sometimes it's a result of something you've done intentionally, but a lot of times things happen that you have no control over. People ask if I'd change anything if I could. It's a waste of time to think about things like that. Your life unfolds on a sheet called "time," and when it's gone, it's gone forever. The best you can do is to learn from your past, and attempt to control your future. As long as you're alive there's a chance, however slim, that you can exert some control over your future actions. The Japanese have a saying, "fall down seven times, get up eight." I fell down many times in my life, but I kept getting up.

When I started writing, I thought it would be hard to come up with things to write about. It's proved to be just the opposite. I've tried to be honest, but I haven't told everything. There are some things I've never told anyone. It would serve no purpose, and I'll take them with me to the grave. I'm sure I've told enough to prove I deserve the title of dumbass. Unfortunately, I'm not the only dumbass in the world. Most everyone is a dumbass to some degree. That's the simple truth. The problem is that not everyone sees that in themselves. Worse yet, they see it but refuse to admit it. If you don't admit it to yourself, you will never learn from your dumbass mistakes.

My friend "Preacher" says her God keeps me going so I can help others to keep getting up. I guess you can tell by now that I'm not big into religion. I've always said religious people scare me because they'll kill you quicker than anybody. Recently there was a television series on CNN called "God's Warriors." It covered the three main religions of the world. They all have one thing in common. They all believe that their "God" is the only legitimate God, and they all have a "book" that tells them this. More importantly, they all say that anyone who doesn't believe the same should be killed. I have a book I try to live by. It's called *Zen and the Martial Arts*. I have read it many times, and I give a copy to my black belts. Basically, it tells how to live a peaceful life by mastering yourself and respecting other human beings. The killing of others is never mentioned. When I was watching people claiming to be "God's warriors," I couldn't help but wonder why any "all powerful God" would need warriors. It seems to me an all powerful being should be able to handle things without anyone's help.

It's really very simple. Don't be a dumbass. Everyone has limits, but you should always try to exceed those limits. There cannot be success without failure. If you have problems, do your best to fix them. Accept responsibility for your actions and learn from them. You cannot change your life overnight. Don't beat yourself up if you fail, just get up and try again. Choose to be a good person.

I do know for sure that there are good people in the world, and there are definitely evil human beings. I think the good ones are that way because their common sense tells them what is right and wrong, and they choose to do the right things. They aren't doing it for some reward in future lives. If they had never heard of God, they would still be decent human beings. As for the evil ones, they too are generally evil by choice. It's convenient for them to blame others for their behavior. The devil made me do it. Everyone has a dark side. As we grow and learn we choose our path. The yin-yang circle is half black and half white. In the middle of the black side there's a small white circle. In the middle of the white side is a small black circle. This signifies that nothing is totally one way. No human is totally good or totally bad. As I've gotten older I've tried to do good things to make up for the bad things. I'm not doing it for some reward in this life or the next. I'm doing it to bring balance and peace to my mind.

Have I succeeded in accomplishing this? I feel like the master who was said to have reached an enlightened state. When asked how it felt to be enlightened, he replied "As miserable as ever." I continue to struggle to control my mind and my actions, and I have good and bad times. I have the scars to remind me of the really bad times. The scars are a good thing. They prove that my past was real. I doubt that anything I do or have done in the past will cause any disruptions in the time line of the future. To those in my past I have hurt in any way, I am truly sorry. I alone accept responsibility for my actions. Have I made up for all the bad things I have done? I don't know. I do know that when I was watching my blood go down the drain, I believed that I had honestly tried my best, and my mind was at peace. I will continue to do the best I can, and if there is a "higher power" that has some influence on my actions, I would appreciate any help I can get. I still believe that I alone control my actions. May God forgive me if I'm wrong.

I've recently quit my job. People ask me if I'm enjoying retirement. At the moment I really don't consider myself retired. I'm just not working at the moment. It'll have to last more than a month before I consider myself retired. I am, however, enjoying the hell out of it. I haven't woken up pissed off since the day I left the pharmacy. I've got a new Corvette, skydiving, going to the gym, tae kwon do, and possibly more writing to keep me occupied. If for some reason I have to go back to work, I'll do it. Anything is possible. If you've read this book, I hope you enjoyed it. If you've seen yourself in some of the dumbass things I have done, I hope it has made you realize that it's possible to change. It's not easy to change. If it was easy everyone would do it. It's easier if you have help and support. My wife and others got me to this point. If you want to change and can't find anyone to help, contact me. I'll help you.

The Beginning of the End

Printed in the United States
151793LV00004B/8/P